*Collecting
Tomorrow's
Collectibles*

D1458107

Collecting

Tomorrow's Collectibles

by Jeffrey Feinman

Collier Books
A Division of Macmillan Publishing Co., Inc.
NEW YORK

Collier Macmillan Publishers
LONDON

Macmillan Publishing Co., Inc.
866 Third Avenue, New York, N.Y. 10022
Collier Macmillan Canada, Ltd.

Library of Congress Cataloging in Publication Data

Feinman, Jeffrey.
    Collecting tomorrow's collectibles.

    1. Antiques.   I. Title.
NK1125.F43   745.1'075   79-21597
ISBN 0-02-080040-1

First Printing 1979

Printed in the United States of America

This book is about
very special things. And
it's dedicated
to very special friends . . .
the Slaters

Contents

PART TWO: A CATALOG OF COLLECTIBLES

Part One: Discovering Tomorrow's Collectibles Today

CHAPTER I

The Pleasures of Collecting

Collecting. The very word conjures up images of bright, sunny walks along the beach, of long winter afternoons spent rummaging through long-forgotten trunks, of walking into some out-of-the-way little secondhand shop and discovering a rare antique. The sparkle and glitter of silver and turquoise jewelry . . . the quaintness and charm of turn-of-the-century bisque dolls . . . the solidity and beauty of early American antique chairs . . . the nostalgia and fun of those first comic books.

No matter how you do it or what you attempt to accumulate, there's a certain pleasure in this hobby that continues to fascinate both novices and experts alike. And once you get started it will continue to captivate your interest. It's one hobby that doesn't require a large initial investment or a lot of time in training before you can start or long, grueling hours of practice.

In fact, you can start collecting almost without realizing that you're doing so, or at least without the purpose of building something great that everyone will want to look at and bid for.

And it can be profitable, too!

Take the case of B. L. Boykin* of Fredericksburg, Virginia. All his life he worked as a hardware dealer, earning an average income. But B. L. Boykin had a passion for antiques.

* All collectors' names in this book have been disguised to protect the collectors, but all stories are true.

So he spent every spare penny on American collectibles. Over the years, he watched his collection soar in value. Today his collection is valued at over $1 million! And he did it all on the money he made as a hardware dealer.

One fascinating footnote: Boykin discovered how to make a handsome extra income from his collection—without selling a single item. Last year, he earned over $70,000—simply by showing his collection to other eager Americana lovers!

How Collections Begin

This is how most collections start. You discover that you have a great interest in literature, for example, so you automatically search through every pile of old books you come across. Eventually you may accumulate several tomes by one author that are old enough to be valuable—hence a worthwhile collection.

You may run across an item that was part of your childhood—an old baseball card, a toy bank, even a Coke bottle—and this may get you interested in finding other related items. Or friends may give you a gift that complements your tastes, such as an antique music box. You like it so well that you want to find other music boxes.

Just about any chance find, unconscious accumulation, or studied area of interest can lead to a collection. Collections have been built because of an interest in history, a search for one's roots, a love of nostalgia, growing attendance at museums, increased leisure time to explore new tastes and trends, the wider range of things that can be collected—as well as the public's increased affluence and desire for monetary gain.

It's Easy to Become Compulsive

Whatever your reason for starting your collection, you will find that it won't be difficult to keep it going. Most people who begin to accumulate items of interest find that what started out as a hobby quickly turns into a habit. So involved do they become in their collection that it's the first thing they turn to in their spare time. At times the act of collecting becomes more important than the collection itself.

Even for those who do not become so compulsive, however, collecting can be an intensely satisfying and personally rewarding experience. It will bring you into a whole new world of people, places, and things. You'll broaden your horizons, make new discoveries, and meet exciting new friends.

The Complete Collector

One thing to keep in mind as you begin (or continue) this venture: Aim to make your collection a totality. There's a very good reason for this. If you have a whole series of different matchboxes (or any other item, for that matter) and if you put a lot of care and consideration into making your collection as varied as possible, your matchboxes will be infinitely more valuable than if you just hoarded all the matchboxes you could dig up without regard for the quality of each individual item in the collection. Generally a total collection will bring much more money—and give a greater sense of satisfaction—than all the items individually.

Once you have begun to form a total collection, you'll also discover something else. Your collection becomes a creative outlet, even a work of art, in itself.

CHAPTER II

The Confessions of a Compulsive Collector

It must have started in my childhood, when my mother told me I couldn't have that Mickey Mouse watch I wanted for my birthday. Mom was never a very good judge of future value. If she had bought that watch when I was eight years old, for a mere $10, I could have sold it today for at least *ten times* the price she would have paid.

So I learned my lesson—and began to collect everything in sight just as soon as I was grown up and had extra money to spend for pleasure. And it began to pay off handsomely.

Making a Profit

While on a trip to Maine, I happened to stop at a church-sponsored auction. A set of blue bubble depression glass was offered. The bidding was practically nonexistent. It seemed nobody realized that depression glass is a collectible. I "stole" that forty-piece place setting for $8—and sold it two days later to a New York City antique dealer for $95. In other words, I made over a thousand percent on my investment.

I also learned a valuable lesson: *The only way a collector makes a profit on his investment is to sell his collection.*

Time and again people have told me that they have a collection worth thousands—even millions—in genuine ancient whatchamacallits. That's balderdash! A collection is only worth something if someone is willing to pay the price. This truly is the test. Your collection must have a resale value and interest to someone other than you.

Special Information

Now let me tell you the next lesson I learned. I was shopping in a local bookstore and happened to see a copy of Marc Chagall's *Illustrations for the Bible* sitting on the shelf like an ordinary book (I happened to know that this particular book is worth well over $2,000). I asked the clerk if he realized this was a truly valuable book. He smiled and said, "Of course." Then he took the book off the shelf and put it in the special section containing rare, expensive books. I looked on the front page—and saw that the price of the book had been changed from $200 to $2,000.

If I hadn't opened my big mouth and told the clerk he had a valuable book, I could have picked up that Chagall volume for $200.

This, then, is lesson number two: *When you have a special piece of information, keep it to yourself.*

That Extra Edge

Now for my next lesson. Three years ago, while on a fishing trip with my friends Debbie and Milt Pierce, I noticed a store that advertised "old books." That was something I just couldn't resist.

When I looked in the store, I noticed a rare first edition of Mark Twain's *Life on the Mississippi*. It was priced at $45, far below the market value. I remembered then that another friend, Steven Grant, once told me he would pay as much as $300 for that same book just to complete his collection of first-edition Mark Twains. It was the only book missing from his Twain collection.

I got that book, and resold it to Mr. Grant for $90. (I

confess that I made a hundred-percent profit on my investment. I even told Grant that at the time. He was thoroughly delighted to get the Twain volume—at any price below $300.)

The lesson I learned from this experience: *When you know that someone is actively interested in getting a particular collectible, you have a special advantage. Don't miss your chance.*

Selling What You Have Bought

The final lesson I am going to relate is perhaps the most important to any serious collector.

It began in Rome, on vacation with George and Barbara Whitfield. Barbara was looking in a little store near the Spanish Steps. She noticed that the store had a wonderful collection of Russian icons.

"These are very much in demand in New York," Barbara told us. "If the price is right, I could make a killing."

The price was right, so Barbara borrowed a few thousand dollars and purchased every icon the store had. She came home to New York carrying a valise packed with Russian icons, over two dozen of them.

She was amazed to find that the market had dropped out of the icon business, and she could not unload them without taking a big loss.

It was a lesson none of us forgot: *You don't have a real killing in the collectible business unless you are absolutely certain that you will be able to sell what you have bought. A transaction takes both a buyer and a seller.*

Over the years I've learned a lot more about the collectible business. It's been a hobby, a business, an avocation, and a joy. I've learned more about business, human nature, and history from this pastime than from just about any other source. Now I want to share these experiences, so that you can enjoy the fun (and the profit) as well.

CHAPTER III

Collections Divers and Sundry

American Indian jewelry . . . English pewter . . . old 78 rpm records . . . early 1960s Beatle cards . . . armor from the Middle Ages . . . ancient Spanish gold coins . . . early American bisque dolls . . . railroad locks from the early days of trains . . . Art Deco furniture . . . first editions of Dickens's works.

All these collections, diverse as they are, have one thing in common: All were put together because their owners enjoyed having them. When you stop to think about it, that's usually how collections get started.

You develop an interest in stamps, let's say. Maybe you once saw an unusual stamp, one that portrayed a historical event. You liked it so much that you decided to look for other stamps with pictures of important events. Eventually you accumulated a large selection of such stamps and began to organize them according to date and country. That's how it happens. You discover something that gives you pleasure. Your pleasure becomes a hobby. And, if you stick with it, your hobby becomes a collection.

Of course, once you get beyond the starting point, you may have to put a lot of effort and time into building your collection. But if you have that initial pleasure in what you're doing, your collection will probably become even more enjoyable as you put more work into it.

That's getting a little ahead of the game, though. What you have to discover first is what you—not your local antique dealer, not the country's foremost expert on rare coins, not even your neighbor across the street who grabs up every arrowhead in sight—but what *you* enjoy. Once you know what you truly like, what makes your day a little happier, what you enjoy sharing with your friends, what you prefer to do in your spare time, when you're on your way to discovering your own personal collection.

To help you evaluate your interests here are some categories around which collections can be built.

Personal Experience

Just about every important moment in your life has an object attached to it. Whether it's a major event like a graduation ceremony or wedding, or the time you went hiking and found an arrowhead on the ground, you have very likely kept some object to remind you of the experience.

You may collect theater programs or ticket stubs, you may have all your friends' signatures scrawled inside the pages of an autograph book, you may store boxes of personal letters. Just about anything can be used to evoke memories of the happiest occasions in your life. Perhaps you have started such a collection without even consciously realizing you were doing so. If so, add to it. You never know when it might be worth money. Of course, even if your collection never brings a cent, it will still be a treasury of memories! But these personal items often do come to have considerable financial value.

Adulation

Objects of adulation are those that once belonged to famous people. They can be as specific as the items of Abraham Lincoln's clothing his wife tried to sell after his death. Or they can be more general, such as the autographs of baseball stars. In either case, this type of collection is one of the more difficult to build up. But if you are absolutely enthralled at every movie Clark Gable ever made (and if you have money enough to find and buy items that once belonged to him), you might attempt to start a collection of his possessions.

Collections of this sort can even be begun with the objects of people who have achieved only a small degree of noteworthiness. You may even want to begin collecting items of people not yet famous. This, of course, is where your good judgment is essential. Consider an amateur photographer by the name of Astrid who started taking pictures of an English rock group while they were trying to make it big in Hamburg, Germany. Today her photos of the Beatles are collectors' items.

Uniqueness

Generally, objects are crafted to high standards of technique and artistry. But occasionally a mistake is made. And the mistake often becomes more valuable than the original intent. Coins struck the wrong way . . . stamps printed upside down . . . dolls made of different materials than their contemporary counterparts . . . a porcelain cup mistakenly made without a handle—all these errors may vastly increase an object's value.

One caution, though: The mistake must be of such unprecedented occurrence that it makes the object valuable. To determine whether the object is worth collecting, find out how many there are and what each is worth. Consult dealers and manufacturers before you buy.

Items Old, Items New

Fortunes have been made at both extremes: the ancient and the ultramodern. If your tastes run to either the very old or the very new, you may want to start a collection of Chinese pottery . . . Celtic art . . . Greek and Roman sculpture . . . the latest fashion clothing . . . movie posters . . . op-art patterns in dishware.

Before you jump whole-hog into this venture, check into the availability of the old or the value of the new. Most, if not all, of the ancient artifacts and art objects of real value are in museums or the private collections of the wealthy. And your collection of the nouveau may eventually do nothing but collect dust. So get the facts before you start.

Old-Fashioned Flavor

Objects in this category are distinguished from their more ancient counterparts by the fact that they're not all that old. But they're not all that new either.

High-button shoes . . . returnable glass soda bottles . . . political buttons . . . your mother's dresses . . . 78 rpm records . . . Shirley Temple dolls . . . twenty-year-old Christmas cards . . . Cracker Jack toys—these are just some of the things used in this century that have disappeared from public view. So look in your attic, think about what you like, and have some good old-fashioned fun.

The Ludicrous

If you have a yen for the humorous, the trivial, or even the absurd, this is your category. Among the things you may want to collect are comic strips, funny greeting cards, metal tabs from soda cans, complicated gadgets that don't work, or just about anything that most people don't consider worth collecting. You are limited only by your imagination.

Status

Collecting is not just an end in itself; it's also an open invitation to high society. If such is your wish, you may want to start collecting items that other people—especially the "right" people—admire. Many of these (art and jewelry, for example) require a fairly large fund of investment capital, but others can be acquired for little money.

Find out what the people you admire enjoy most, and then start collecting it. Ideally, you should also enjoy what you're collecting. It may become more difficult to add to your collection if your only motivation is to please others. Other people's tastes may change without your being aware of it.

A collection can become a common bond between yourself and the glamorous few. In fact, after you have become fairly expert in your personal collection, you may even be able to serve as an adviser to one of the very rich who has the same interest.

Career Collectibles

The jockey who lives, breathes, and sleeps horses is very likely to build his collection around horses as well. Not just horses in the flesh but horse statues, horses on canvas, horses on plates, horses on scarves—in fact, horses on anything. The same can be true of almost any occupation. The musician collects not only instruments but sheet music, paintings and prints of the master composers, records, music boxes, music stands, et cetera. But you don't have to be in a given field to build a collection on it. Even outmoded occupations, such as blacksmithing, are good ones for collectors.

Practicality

The first collectors of fine furniture were not antique dealers but the nobility. And they didn't use it as a hedge against inflation. Instead they sat on it, ate from it, even slept on it. The lavish beds, cabinets, bookcases, desks, tables, and chairs that we can see only in museums today were once pieces of everyday furniture.

The same can be true in your home. If you appreciate having a clock in every room, you may want to go to some trouble to make your clock collection as valuable as possible. If you're constantly giving dinner parties, you may want to search for the exotic or the rare in dinnerware. This goes for just about anything you use every day, from chairs to books to radios to watches—even telephones.

Ancestry

This type of collection involves a little more than a personal interest. To start, you must be able to find out something about your parents, grandparents, great-grandparents, and so on back down your ancestral line. You may know, for instance, that your great-grandmother kept a scrapbook of pictures and other family mementos; perhaps, by digging a little in the attic, you can find your grandmother's and your mother's photos and add them to your great-grandmother's collection. Or you may want to discover the family crests. (This is an especially important industry in Britain.) What you do with your collection depends on you—and your family. If your collection has historical value, it could, for instance, greatly enhance a museum exhibit.

World View

Keeping an eye out for the exotic, the quaint, or even the slightly unusual can do wonders for your collection and increase the enjoyment you get out of traveling. In many countries the rush to buy up anything of value has not yet hit, and there are still bargains to be found.

In many cases you may discover items you like that have somehow escaped popularity. Whether it's handcrafted knick-knacks, original Eskimo art, antique musical instruments, or silk kimonos, you may find it waiting at your next stop.

Of course, you shouldn't limit your search to the rest of

the world. Even here in the U.S., there are a number of un-tapped attics, out-of-the-way garage sales, and small junk shops. One of them may have just what you're looking for.

Personal Need

This last category is a much more elusive and individual one. Here the motives for building a collection are twofold: healing and growth.

The boy who never was good enough to make the Little League may try to compensate for his failure by collecting baseball bats, gloves, or even cards. The same holds true for any situation in which you are frustrated or handicapped; having a collection can be a very positive way to turn dis-appointment into achievement.

A collection can also be a means of learning, a key to increasing your understanding and abilities. The antique instruments collector, for example, may want to learn how to play the instruments in his collection. Collecting old railroad memorabilia—train locks, switching gears, benches from old train stations—may help one to understand the importance of trains in America's history. And so on.

There's another value to collecting. It enables you to escape from the tensions of daily life, to find needed relaxation. Practically anything you collect can enrich your life far beyond its monetary value. So grow with your collection—and happy hunting.

CHAPTER IV

Strategy

Focusing Your Collection

You've decided to become a collector. You even have some ideas of what you want to collect. Your next step, then, is to narrow down your ideas until you discover *exactly* what you want.

If you're going to be a stamp collector, will you collect all stamps or just those from a certain country, say, the United States? Will you search for stamps printed a hundred years ago or stay with those still being used today? These are just two of the many questions the stamp collector should answer before beginning a collection.

You get the point. You can't just say you're going to collect bottles, for instance. If you do, you'll wind up with a cellarful of glass containers that have no relationship to each other. To make some sense of your collection, as well as to obtain some profit from it, you have to know exactly what you want to collect: the specific type, quality, size, age, et cetera, of your bottles. Once you know what you want, you'll know what to look for.

Here are some ways you might decide to focus your collection:

Historical period: Items from a certain era, such as Coke bottles from the 1930s and 40s, can form the basis of a collection. Make sure the time period you choose is long enough to give you an adequate supply of objects and short enough to keep your collection manageable.

Similarity and comparison: All nutcrackers crack nuts, but they don't all do it in the same way. So if you decide to collect nutcrackers try to find as many different kinds as you can. The key here is finding a collection that is basically similar in one point (i.e., cracking nuts), yet different in many others (structure of nutcracker, method used, et cetera). Or you may have a collection of similar objects with only one difference, say, bottles with different types of corks.

Change: In this category, you could work with either a short time period or a long one—depending on what you are collecting. If you want to show how model cars have changed, for instance, your time period will be shorter than if your subject is jewelry or dishes. Your purpose will be the same either way: You will try to show what changes have occurred in the item you collect.

Special features: Included in this category might be necklaces or bracelets with a certain type of clasp, plates with butterflies on them, paisley-print quilts, et cetera. The key here is selecting only those items that have the special feature you've chosen.

Complete set: The item you want to collect (say, U.S. silver dollars) may already be organized in a set. If so, your job is to find and purchase all the items in the set. Coins, magazines, newspapers, limited-edition artworks, and first-edition books are some of the items that fall into this category.

Materials: This type of collection is defined by the material the objects are made of. Copper, gold, silver, brass, steel, jade, ivory, even tin—each one is used to make different types of objects. If you have a special affinity for copper, you may want to build your collection around objects made from it: jewelry, cooking pots, or sculpture, for example. The same can be done with all other materials. (Of course, some materials—such as gold or jade—may be prohibitively expensive, but others are generally affordable.)

Once you have focused your collection, the next step is to find out how and where you can obtain the items you want.

Building Your Collection

This second step in collecting is slightly more difficult. Now you have to go out and find what you want. You will notice I said "find," not "buy." That's because there are a number of ways to pick up items for your collection without having to pay top money for them.

To start, let's look at some sources of free merchandise:

Fields and beaches: These are a valuable source, not only for nature collections (shells, rocks, arrowheads, leaves, flower petals), but also for small items that people may easily drop (coins, cans and bottles, keys).

Garbage dumps: Almost anything and everything can be found here, but it's best to search only for more common items. In other words, you probably won't find dinosaur bones, gold jewelry, and Rembrandt paintings in trash heaps.

Attics, cellars, and garages: These are a very rich source for collections, especially if they haven't been cleaned out in some time. Neighbors and friends may let you have some or all of the items you want in exchange for doing the cleaning.

Letters: You can often obtain free items simply by writing away for them. Autographs, postage stamps (writing to a foreign country will automatically bring you a foreign stamp), and free booklets are just some of the things you can collect through the mail. (For example, I've built a huge collection of foreign stamps by asking my banker to save them for me.) *Your own house:* Your own possessions may already form a previously unnoticed collection. Or you may own valuable items you can exchange for what you want.

Flea markets: Many dealers and sellers will barter, if they like your merchandise. This can save you some cash.

Secondhand shops: If you can get a job in one of these, the owner may be willing to pay you in merchandise rather than money.

Condemned buildings: Many might already have been stripped of anything valuable, but it's always good to take a look just in case something you want was left behind. In case of possible legal restrictions, check with the owner and/or police before entering the building.

Household sales: This source is not exactly free, but many times you can find what you want for next to nothing. Since most people are selling their possessions just to get rid of them, they're likely to agree to any price you name.

At the expensive end of the market spectrum, of course, are the dealers, auctions, and large private collectors. After you have established your collection, you may find it helpful or necessary to go to these more expensive sources. But in many cases you should be able to start your collection for little or nothing.

Researching Your Collection

There are two basic sources of information on your field of interest: verbal and written. Both are prone to inaccuracies; but if you have many sources you can check them against each other and come up with a fairly good idea of how and what to collect.

Verbal sources include owners of items you would like to collect, dealers, museum curators and other museum personnel, sponsors of auctions and exhibitions, and sometimes even store clerks, flea market operators, and owners of secondhand shops.

When asking anyone about an item you're interested in, keep two things in mind:

The speaker probably has at least some personal interest in the object. You must carefully weigh the information you receive, particularly if you are planning to buy the object from the person you're speaking with. Any seller aims to get the best possible price, and some sellers don't mind misrepresenting their merchandise in order to increase their profits. So be cautious and get the facts from more than one dealer or expert. Often, just a little bit of time could save a lot of money.

The more questions you ask, the more information you'll receive. Ask questions designed to generate information, rather than questions that require only a yes or no answer. A question like "Is it valuable?" is not as helpful as "How valuable is it?"

You should also have a large store of written information at your disposal. Check your local library for sources on your subject of interest. Visit dealers and ask for their recommendations on reference books. Check area bookstores for their collections on collections. Don't neglect the extensive, well-researched information available at museum and university libraries. In general, both these sources are open to the public and free of charge.

If you don't find what you're looking for, ask where you *can* find it. You should read as much as you can about your collection before you go out and purchase items for it.

Once you have done some initial research, don't stop learning. Subscribe to collectors' magazines, continue to visit the library for updated information, join collectors' organizations, and keep visiting your favorite dealers and experts. Your collection is only as good as what you put into it, so your research should continue as long as you are a collector.

Organizing Your Collection

The organization of your collection begins the moment you buy your first item. At the time you purchase an item for your collection, ask for a bill of sale. This bill should list the date of sale, characteristics of the item (age, condition), and amount paid. *Keep the bill for insurance and resale purposes.*

After the item has been transported to its place of storage, make a record of it. This record should include all the information listed on the bill of sale, plus an identification number (you'll probably want to number each item in the order you acquire it), the item's source, condition, description, and current location. When and if you sell the item, you should add to this record the name of the new owner, the date sold, and the price received.

Photograph each item for insurance and identification purposes. If it is lost or stolen, photos could help recover it. Also, mark each item with your own special seal or with the electric engravers available from most police stations. If there's any doubt as to your ownership of an item, the mark will settle the question.

Two other important aspects of organizing are security and insurance. When you first purchase an item, consider the safest place to store it and have it transported there immediately. Your collection of antique dolls might be safe in a locked display cabinet in your home, but that is certainly not the place for gold coins! Bank vaults, museums, and galleries are all secure places to store your collection, and the added security is usually well worth any fees you have to pay for storage.

For those items that you plan to keep at home, it is wise to display or store them inside a locked cabinet. You may also want to install a burglar alarm in the cabinet. But when you're away, make sure the collection is taken to a safer place for storage.

If your local police precinct has such a policy, give them a list of your valuables and their location. In case of a robbery this could give the police a jump on any intruders.

Another major factor to consider is insurance. If your collection has any monetary value at all, it should be insured. You may want to have your regular insurance agent call in an expert on your particular collection, so you can discuss the type and amount of insurance needed. The insurance covering your collection may be included in your current homeowner's policy, or it may be a separate policy.

Before you purchase any insurance, be sure to have an outside appraiser determine the exact value of your collection. Then know exactly under what conditions the insurance company will pay you. Will your policy cover damages from moving, storms, or official inspection; depreciation or wear and tear; damage as a result of repairs or restoration; breakage of part or all of the collection? If you insure the total collection but lose only a part of it, will you have to give what remains to the insurance company in order to receive payment? These are just some of the questions only your insurance agent can answer. Make sure to ask them and get clear answers, in writing.

These are just some general tips to help organize, protect, and guarantee your collection. If you require more specific information related to any particular item, consult a local museum or expert in that field. Above all, don't buy any item until you know exactly how you're going to take care of it.

Preserving and Displaying Your Collection

Once you have your collection organized and insured, there are certain things you can do to enhance and maintain its value. Preserving your collection is absolutely essential if you are to maintain its aesthetic and monetary value. The exact repairs, restoration techniques, and cleaning procedures will vary with the type of item.

The first step in preserving your valuables is simply a matter of common sense. Handle everything with care. In general, use both hands when holding any small item and lift, rather than push, when moving a large item. Never touch paintings on the front or back; instead, move them by holding both edges with both hands. To handle any object made of metal, place a glove or cloth between the object and your hands. (Don't allow your guests to to touch parts of your collection unless they know how to handle them or unless you are willing to risk having something damaged or broken.)

Where and how you display your collection, if you choose to display it, is largely a matter of what you collect, how valuable it is, and what space you have available. For items that can safely be kept in your home, you will probably want to have a lighted glass display case or cabinet, perhaps lined with a cloth in a matching or contrasting color to brighten the display.

If you choose not to put your collection inside a cabinet or case, you must be careful to place it where it cannot be knocked over, spilled on, or easily stolen by some not-so-welcome guest. Some collectors go to great pains to fasten down any item they wish to keep outside a case. Keeping an object out in the open also requires more frequent cleaning and increases the risk of breakage, so it is generally not advisable.

Most of the time your collection will probably be stored where it's displayed. For those times when it has to be kept elsewhere, you should keep the following points in mind: humidity, ventilation, wrapping, protection against fire, insects and mildew, lighting and temperature.

Although every item differs with respect to the light, temperature, humidity, ventilation, and protection it requires, in general, all objects should be covered to keep dust out and should not be stored in any place where the temperature is above 72°F. or below 50°F. Paper items should never be covered with newspaper; this will only ruin your collection (newspaper attracts bugs). Because metal shelves conduct heat, they are not the fire protectors one might think; if you wish to use them, cover them with felt. (Some experts believe wooden cabinets are the best storage places; even if they are burned on the outside, their contents often remain undamaged). Musical instruments require some circulation of air. Cloth items should generally be rolled rather than folded, and of course they must be protected against moths and mildew.

Here is a general guideline for proper humidity:

55% humidity is best for wood, paintings, ivory, and leather
50% is best for paper and plaster
45% is best for ceramics
40% is best for metals, cloth, and glass

Since practically anything can be a collectible, storage requirements vary greatly. Thorough research of your particular collection will give you more information on how best to care for it.

CHAPTER V

Six Tragic Tales

John Winston has the largest collection of Mickey Mouse memorabilia in Paramus, New Jersey. There's only one problem: He also has the *only* collection of Mickey Mouse memorabilia in Paramus. Therefore, in order to trade or even talk about his collection, he has to go fifty miles away, to New York City. John discovered the first thing to look for when starting a collection: There should be a lot of interest in the same type of collection in the area where you are now living.

Jan Ritter has the greatest collection of Deanna Durbin movie posters in Crown Heights, Brooklyn. As a matter of fact, she has the only collection of Deanna Durbin movie posters in the world. Jan is truly a unique character, and her collection is one of a kind. That's the problem: There's nobody else in the world interested in Deanna Durbin movie posters except Jan Ritter. Even though she has a fabulous collection, she has something that nobody else is really interested in.

Dr. Harwood Fisher has spent thousands of dollars in collecting pre-twentieth-century stethoscopes. His collection is valuable and historic. But it is not complete. As a matter of fact, it is virtually impossible to complete. Dr. Fisher's problem is quite simple: He started something that he can never complete.

Judy Michael read an ad for the Historic Old Parsippany Mint. They were issuing a beautiful collection of coins commemorating the world's greatest musical comedies. "This is a strictly limited edition," the advertisement declared, "and is virtually guaranteed to go up in value."

Judy paid $185 per coin, and amassed a collection of seventy-five coins. (There have been an awful lot of musical comedies, she discovered!) The total cost of her collection was $13,875.

"This is something that will grow in value," she thought. "Something to keep for my old age."

Alas, Judy discovered that the coins were worth only $3,000 when she tried to sell them—a loss of over $10,000. Why? Because she failed to read the small print. When the ad said that these coins were "virtually" guaranteed to go up in value, there was no *real* guarantee. And when the ad said that this was a limited edition, it did not say that the edition was limited to the first fifty-thousand people who bought the coins.

Some guarantee! Some limited edition!

Now let me tell you the story of Joe England. He also bought one of those sets of commemorative coins. Joe thought that it would be wise to get the coins in genuine silver. "After all," he thought, "silver has gone up over three hundred percent in the past ten years." So he took a lot of money out of the bank and purchased a set of coins commemorating the great battles of the Franco-Prussian War.

He was due for a rude awakening. It's true that silver has gone up by over 300 percent. But Joe England was paying $89.56 for each coin, and each coin weighed less than an ounce. Good old Joe was paying over ten times the cost of the raw metal. If he wanted to buy silver for investment purposes, he should have purchased ingots—at the cost of the metal—and not coins.

Consider Kathy Fowler. She, too, decided to invest half her life savings in a set of commemorative coins. The ad, from the Historic Old Manhattan Mint, was glowing in its promises. She read the ad again and again. "This investment is guaranteed to go up in value by at least 35% a year . . . and if you do not agree that this is the best investment that you have ever made in your entire lifetime, just let us know— and we will guarantee to buy back each and every coin at the full price you have paid."

There was no possible way that Kathy Fowler could lose a cent, right? Wrong!

When she decided that she wanted her money back, Kathy Fowler had her rude awakening. She mailed her coins back to the Historic Old Manhattan Mint in a fully insured package. In a few days, the package was returned. Kathy's hands shook with indignation as she read the bright red message stamped on the outside of the package:

"THIS COMPANY IS NO LONGER IN BUSINESS. THEY FILED BANK-RUPTCY IN 1976."

Kathy, Joe, Judy, Harwood, Jan, and John—all leaped into their investments without looking, and their collecting dreams turned into nightmares.

Now that you have heard these six tragic tales, now that you understand collecting has pitfalls as well as pleasures, please: *Don't let this happen to you!*

What Not to Collect

Just as it's important to know what to collect, it's equally important to know what *not* to collect. There are closets filled with so-called investments that will never return a fraction of the price paid. The classic investment mistakes fall into a few specific categories.

1. *Widely available at original price.* From coast to coast there are safe-deposit boxes stuffed with U.S. postage stamps. Though certain commemorative issues are available, most are not. Sadly, most will never be worth more

than the face value charged by the post office. With issues in the hundreds of millions, the supply will always exceed the demand.

2. *Artificially created collectibles.* So-called private mints create instant collectibles, often numbered and commemorating a special event. Although they are gold, silver, or gold electroplate, the metallic value is a fraction of the selling price. Therefore, a $50 item may fetch $20 or less from a dealer even a decade later.

3. *Limited-interest collectibles.* A close friend collects ashtrays with birds on them. If he enjoys them, that's fine. However, it is unlikely such collection will find resale value, since its appeal is limited.

4. *Mass-produced merchandise.* Since a single run of *TV Guide* is twenty million copies, it's unlikely that any will ever appreciate, unless there is something special about the issue. Similarly, although you shouldn't bother saving most current *Playboy* magazines, the issue with the Jimmy Carter interview will fetch high prices in future years. By the same token, old Coca-Cola bottles are worthwhile, yet the current version is stamped out daily in the millions.

5. *Perishable items or those that store poorly.* The last edition of the *New York Daily Mirror* is worthwhile, yet newspapers deteriorate quickly. If you invest in perishable collectibles, be careful with them. Usually they're better to avoid altogether.

6. *Items that have already had huge price increases and have no intrinsic value.* It's unlikely that certain collectibles will continue their growth rate. Everything has a ceiling. In the 1600s in Holland certain tulip bulbs brought thoussands of dollars, and suddenly they were worth pennies. It's all too easy to get caught up in the frenzy of collecting. If a tin cookie box was worth $1 in 1950, $10 in 1960, and $250 today, it might be worth stopping and saying "Isn't this crazy?" Invest in items that have not already skyrocketed.

CHAPTER VI

The Investment Potential of Collectibles

Ten years ago, antique buff Jim Noyes paid $1.98 for a Dick Tracy watch. Today that same watch is worth over $200. This kind of situation happens every day.

It's not only diamonds, gold, and art masterpieces that are climbing in value; it's the toys, comic books, banks, records, and even fad items that were in almost every household ten, twenty, or thirty years ago. Items that sold for under $5 when they were originally made may now go for hundreds, even thousands of dollars. How can you be sure that the same thing will happen to your collection? What should you do to make sure that what you collect will be financially as well as aesthetically profitable?

Probably the most important thing you can do before you collect anything (or at least before you pay for anything) is to discover its investment potential. This means discovering that particular collectible's past history in the market: approximately how much the item has been worth each year . . . if and when the price increased significantly . . . how its worth has kept up with inflation . . . if there have been slight or even large drops in the price . . . and other financial data concerning that collectible. You can find this information by consulting books and periodicals on your particular collectible and by asking dealers, appraisers, and other experts.

Once you have this knowledge at your fingertips, you'll

have a fairly good idea of what you're going to have to put into your investment, as well as what you can expect to get out of it.

Most collectors find that their hobby becomes an excellent hedge against inflation. In fact, that's one reason why collecting has become so popular. Seventy, sixty, fifty, even just thirty years ago, the only people who spent much time collecting anything were the superrich, the Rockefellers, Carnegies, and other members of high society who wanted to surround themselves with the best of everything. Even then collectibles were pretty much limited to ancient artifacts, established masterpieces in art, gold and other precious metals and gems, or antiques at least a hundred years old—all items that required hundreds of thousands, even millions of dollars to obtain.

But in the mid-1950s, when people became more affluent, collecting came to be seen more and more as a means of fighting inflation and making money. Sure, there were and are those who collected for the sheer love of their hobby; but increasingly people began to scoop up objects for the potential financial profit they could bring. This trend became self-fulfilling. The more people who went into collecting for financial gain, the greater the financial gain, at least for those who invested wisely.

In this decade investing against inflation has become an even more popular and profitable reason for building a collection. In general, serious collectibles (that is, those that appeal to a wide range of collectors and those that have consistently had some financial value) have risen regularly in price every single year for the past twenty years. This has occurred in times of economic recession as well as upsurge, a fairly good indication that collectibles will continue to reap profits for years to come.

FACT: The 1895 Christmas plate, "The Frozen Window," sold for about 60¢ when it was issued. Today that same plate is worth over $3,000. And there are over four million plate collectors who are eagerly buying up nearly everything that's offered.

FACT: Rare books and manuscripts have risen a steady 25 to 30 percent each year for the past fifteen years. Investors claim that this is the best way to fight inflation and recession.

FACT: A 1932 Roosevelt-Garner election button was sold at auction recently for $100. You could have gotten thousands of them, absolutely free, just forty years ago!

FACT: In 1971 Rosenthal issued a special plate, "Madonna and Child," for $100. Today you cannot get a copy of that Christmas plate for less than $1,500.

FACT: You could buy Action Comics #One for about 25¢ a mere twenty-five years ago. Today the price is $525.

FACT: Tin banks, made by the Marx Toy Company, sold for less than $2 when they were issued a mere three decades ago. Today the price is anywhere from $200 (a bargain!) to well over $700.

FACT: Collectors are just about everywhere, and they collect the most outlandish things. Records . . . toys . . . comics . . . old radio tubes . . . auto hubcaps . . . old photographs . . . even barbed wire!

FACT: Debbie Roth bought a copy of Marc Chagall's *Drawings for the Bible* in 1960. She paid $14 for the book. Today she has been offered over $1,000—and she's holding out for more.

But there are also certain financial disadvantages to investing in collectibles.

1. They pay no dividends or interest. All the time you're holding your precious set of antique glass candlesticks, they're not earning a penny for you.

2. Unlike stocks and bonds, collectibles require a con-

tinual outpouring of your money in insurance, transportation, storage, security, and refinishing costs. This amount has to be taken into consideration when determining how much profit your collection will yield.

3. Unscrupulous dealers, merchants, and peddlers of all kinds have taken advantage of the public interest in collectibles to hawk their own fakes and flawed items. You must be very sure that your money goes for the real thing.

4. Although prices for collectibles in general have risen steadily, individual items may still decrease in value from year to year. Know the market record of your particular collectible before you buy. Don't assume that every item will go along with the general trend.

5. Auctioneers' fees, dealers' wholesale prices, and the general expenses involved in every transaction may significantly cut your profits when you sell.

6. Some economists and investment experts say the prices of certain collectibles are so high that they're bound to fall dramatically in the next few years.

It all adds up to a somewhat confusing picture. Although collectibles have been a truly sensational investment over the years, certain items have not held up in value. The overall picture has been, on the average, far better than the Dow-Jones Industrial Average of the New York Stock Exchange. However, like issues on the Exchange (or any other risky investment), there are winners in a losing market and losers in a winning market. There are fads, trends, and unpredictable events.

In other words, an investment in collectibles is very much like any other investment.

CHAPTER VII

Criteria for Collecting

What items that are sold for a dollar today will be worth thousands of dollars tomorrow? There are no guarantees. However, our recent experiences, as well as conversations with dozens of experts (including the "king" of the auction galleries, George Lowry of Swann; Irv Mayer of the National Bureau of Collectors and Traders; and Sam Ritter, publisher of *The Collector's Course*), led us to establish the following six criteria:

1. IS IT REALLY A SPECIAL ITEM?

    Collectors generally like anything that is different in some way from any predecessor. If a particular collectible is unique in looks, in subject matter, in the material of which it is made, or in any other fundamental respect, collectors will consider it more seriously.

2. IS IT REALLY A LIMITED EDITION?

    Of course, an item must not be too scarce or it will never be commonly known and sought. For an item to be successful, the number of the edition must only be markedly lower than the number of collectors willing to pay good money to get the item.

3. IS IT A GENUINE FIRST ISSUE?

    Almost invariably, the first issue in a series outperforms

all others. Collectors prize first issues; some collect nothing else.

4. DOES IT HAVE AESTHETIC APPEAL?
   With the number of collectors' items increasing, the basic appeal of the item seems of mounting significance. To become popular, any item needs strong appeal, or wide appeal, or both.

5. IS THE PRICE RIGHT?
   Generally, higher prices indicate higher value, but this is not always the case. You should know the average price range of your collectible, how much the condition of the item can change its value, and what its market record has been in the past thirty to forty years.

6. DOES IT HAVE GOOD EARLY SALES?
   With more and more collectors aware that potentially profitable collectibles often sell out early, more take care to buy early. If one dealer says a new item is selling fast, this means little; but if several dealers repeat the thought, prompt action may well be in order.

CHAPTER VIII

What Makes an Item Valuable?

There are price guides available. There are professional, impartial appraisers. There are auctions where prices are public knowledge. All these sources help establish and help you to discern current prices for all kinds of collectibles. But when it comes to paying money out of your own pocket, only you can make the decision as to whether the item's value is worth the asking price. The prices paid for the same type of item are as varied as the collectors who buy them.

How do you know if a price is low, reasonable, or high? How do you know when and where to get the best deal for the least money? Finding appropriate answers to these questions is largely a matter of your own research.

To guide your research, keep in mind certain factors that make an item worth owning: limited and unlimited editions; timing of purchase or sale; beauty; skill in crafting; supply and demand; value of the materials; condition; age; name-dropping; wholesale vs. retail; size.

Limited and Unlimited Editions

The first thing you must learn about this category is that the phrase "limited edition" does not always mean that a very small quantity of the item was produced. The words have been misused frequently in recent years, so don't let any dealer use them on you as an excuse for jacking up the price. (Most reputable dealers won't.) Any item that is *truly* part of a limited edition is usually documented, and you can find out the exact quantity made. If you have any doubts, continue your research before you buy. Unless and until you are thoroughly sure that an item is actually a limited edition, you must assume that it's not, and make your offer accordingly.

Timing

If your local museum is planning a special exhibition on turn-of-the-century clothing, you can be sure that dealers and private collectors with such collections will jack up their prices. Current books and articles on such collections will also tend to boost prices, as will auctions and newspaper stories. In all such cases the best thing you can do is wait until the publicity dies down and hope the prices die down with it. Conversely, if you haven't heard anything relating to your collection for some time, it may be a good time to add to it, while interest is low.

Beauty

This is, naturally, a fairly elusive category; what is beauty to you may be trash to your neighbor. However, in most types of collections a certain standard of aesthetic value has been established. Your job now becomes deciding how well this particular piece fits that standard as well as your own. The mere fact that something meets a general standard of appeal is no reason you should buy it. If you don't like the way it looks, by all means leave it alone. The reverse is also true: If you really appreciate the item, don't worry about what the general public thinks.

Skill in Crafting

The basic question you have to answer here is "How well is this object made?" Does it have flaws that other objects of its type are without? Is it an item that is easily and frequently made—or something that can no longer be manufactured? Again, a thorough knowledge of your field will help answer these questions.

Supply and Demand

As you study your particular collection, you will probably get some indication of what the market for it is and has been. This type of economic research is an ongoing process and is essential to developing a worthy collection. You must know whether your specialty is one that is in short supply with high demand or vice versa. Does the supply/demand ratio vary from year to year, from decade to decade, or from epoch to epoch? In the balance between supply and demand, scarcity lies at one extreme and glut at the other, but it is unlikely that you will be dealing with either extreme.

Value of the Materials

Many objects are valuable, or have added value, simply because of the materials they're made of. Gold, silver, diamonds, ivory, exquisite woods, silk—these are just a few of the materials that have been highly valued throughout history and will probably continue to be valued. The key here is to make sure you're actually getting what you think you're getting. If there's any doubt, call in an impartial appraiser.

Condition

It is generally, but not necessarily, true that the best condition brings the best price. The noted exception is the untouched antique; it will generally sell at a far higher price than one that has been refinished or repaired.

Age

It is not always true that the older the object is, the more money it brings. But there are so few exceptions that it may be considered a general rule. Part of the reason is scarcity. By the time a few hundred years roll around, most objects of an earlier era have long since bitten the dust. Those that remain, therefore, are especially valued, often for sheer survival alone. However, before you attempt to buy up as many ancient manuscripts or old coins, or antique anything, as you can find, follow those two suggestions: (1) Make sure the item is actually as old as the seller says it is, and (2) make sure that the age of the object actually makes it valuable.

Name-Dropping

A Chagall print will usually bring a higher price on the market than a print by one of his protégés. And, if the print has been owned by someone in high society, that fact is likely to drive the price still higher. You get the point. Who created the object, as well as who owned it, has a considerable impact on the object's value. The art collection of Nelson Rockefeller will probably bring a higher-than-usual price, simply because many people will jump at the chance to have something he once owned. The main point to keep in mind when you're faced with the opportunity to snatch up a "name" item is to be sure that the name actually created or owned it. It could be a dealer gimmick, so proceed carefully.

Wholesale vs. Retail

This economic factor applies to practically everything you buy, but when you're dealing with high-priced collectibles, the difference can mean thousands of dollars. Unfortunately, most collectors can only obtain their items (at least in the more expensive antique, stamp, and coin fields) through dealers. That means they are buying from people who pay wholesale and sell retail. It also explains why dealers are often unwilling to pay much for or even to buy your valuables; they must be able to sell them at a higher price in order to make a profit. This also explains why it is often hard for you to get the catalog price when you sell items in your collection. If you frequently sell items in your collection, however, you may be able to buy directly from wholesalers. In some cases your business card may be sufficient entry into wholesale establishments.

Size

You may think this is a strange factor to consider in purchasing your collection, but, especially in economically difficult times, it could mean the difference between keeping your fortune and being stuck with something you can't get rid of. Obviously, if you need to sell right away, a small collection of gold coins would be far more valuable to you than a whole roomful of Elizabethan furniture. Note that throughout history many a person's fortune and livelihood has been saved because of an easily transported collection of jewelry or gold and silver coins.

Even in times of economic growth and stability, size is still a factor. Naturally, larger items require greater space, and often this space has to be rented or purchased. Smaller items, on the other hand, can usually be kept in your home, provided that your insurance and security procedures are adequate. This may be one reason for the recent growth of interest in miniatures. Just be sure that you have room (or can find room) for your collection before you buy or add to it.

CHAPTER IX

Organizing Your Collection

Organizing your collection will help to insure its safekeeping. This means marking it, recording its purchase, and insuring it.

Mark It

To begin, the collector may want to mark each new acquisition with a special code or insignia that only he can recognize.

Although collectors disagree as to whether or not discreet identifying marks will devalue the cost of a collectible, such markings are usually effective safeguards against loss or misplacement. If you do decide to mark your collectibles, do so as follows:

1. Use artist's old colors, cadmium red and vermilion, to mark glass, metal, ceramics, or wood.
2. Use a medium lead pencil to mark paper objects.
3. Use small stitches or liner tape to mark rugs, textiles.
4. Use small rubber stamps, with dark-brown printer's ink, to mark a name or monogram on the reverse side of prints.
5. Use a number to mark small and lightweight objects near their bases.
6. Use a number, on the reverse lower corner or the

reverse upper left corner, of stretchers and frames, to mark hanging or stacked paintings.

7. Mark scroll paintings on the knob of the scroll.

8. Use lacquer thinner to make marks adhere better on smooth surfaces.

9. Use shellac over markings, to protect them, after markings have dried.

10. Certain collectibles, such as coins and stamps, must be absolutely untarnished to achieve greatest dollar value. For these items, use holders and mark as indicated in #2. The most common holders are made of cardboard, with see-through plastic centers, and are available at almost any coin store.

Collectors do agree on two things. When marking an object, never use anything indelible. And, finally, remember to note all markings in your records.

Record It

Records, by virtue of their composition, are infinite repositories of knowledge. They remember the hows, wheres, and whys, otherwise forgotten, about each item in every collection. By timelessly telling its story, a detailed record adds dimension to any acquisition. Well-kept records are tedious and time-consuming, but expedient to the protection of a collection. In case of loss due to theft or catastrophe, records will provide accurate and immediate accounts for the necessary authorities.

Purchase records and receipts are essential to the worth of a collection. They authenticate. As with all records, several copies of these should be made and stored separately. Original purchase records should be cached with other valuable papers.

Keep your records in register, dossier, or file-folder forms. Curio collectors will want to emphasize individual characteristics and specifics, but the form used by most museums to record collectibles includes, in the following order:

1. Identification (or accession) number. This is the individual number given to each entry. Decimals are given for each piece. Small letters are used for each removable part. Example: 64.7a might be a wine decanter with six matching glasses, the stopper being the removable part (a).

2. Place of purchase.

3. Date of purchase.

4. Description. In recording the description of an item, all factors are essential. List imperfections, traces of wear, repairs, and markings.

5. Condition.

6. Cost or estimated value.

7. Location in house.

8. Function.

9. Disposition (when item is sold, leased, or loaned to another collection).

10. Measurements. Record them sequentially: length, width, and depth.

For additional identification, attach a photograph to its corresponding record. Or, marked accordingly, a photograph is a unique and efficient record in itself.

Secure and Insure It

Despite precautions taken to mark and record collections, losses are an inevitable hazard. For this reason, many super-collectors prefer to remain "anonymous." Other private collectors, choose to discourage even the awareness that a collection exists.

It is recommended that inquiries about your collection from an unknown source be turned away. Also, strangers asking to see your collection should be carefully screened. When home security is inadequate, parts of a collection may be stored in warehouses or bank vaults. Otherwise, the normal precautions, taken by any judicious homeowner to secure his property, are sufficient.

Prudent insurance is a normal precaution. Overinsurance is as bad as none at all, as these are the figures used at the time of death to determine estate taxes. For maximum protection efficiency, consult with a specially experienced insurance agent. Most insurance companies offer a "fine arts" policy along with a "master" policy. It is to the collector's advantage to have both policies handled by the same company.

Fine arts policy rates are flexible and depend on circumstances rather than on predetermined risks. Tell the issuing company what you can about your collection. Separately value and list each item. Where it is kept, who handles it, and who sees it will affect the rates you pay.

Frequently excluded from the fine arts policy are coverages for breakage; gradual deterioration; damage from repair or restoration; damage from wear, storm or flood; and damage due to quarantine regulations or government confiscation. Knowing about such exclusions is as important as knowing about the coverage.

The collector who lends his collection, or donates his collection for tax purposes but still retains a part of it, should also consider a legal liability insurance plan for maximum personal protection.

Moving It

The best protection for most collections is simply to be left alone. Though transportation is at best avoided, when it is necessary employ a competent and highly recommended fine arts packer and shipper. Be there to check the condition of your valuables when they reach their destination. If there are damages, make all claims, accompanied by photographs, as promptly as possible.

If you must transport your collection without professional movers, get advice and do the following:

1. Be sure the box you pack measures at least 2½ inches more than the largest object in it.

2. Pack light and heavy objects separately. When this is not possible, use slats to divide the box into compartments.

3. Pack against water damage by securing a waterproof liner to the box. Pack individual pieces in waterproof containers.

4. Bury fine objects in resilient materials. Wrap small, fragile ceramic pieces in tissue and cotton, then float on shredded paper or plastic in individual containers.

5. Screw box covers in place when using a wooden crate. Do not nail.

6. Strap or band-close all boxes being shipped abroad.

7. Mark your box "FRAGILE! THIS END UP!"

Unpacking requires as much attention as packing does. Do not unpack when you are tired. Make diagrams to describe each piece's enclosure and store with outer wrappings for future repacking. You can learn to pack by reading the shipping and trade magazines for the latest packing techniques.

No one precaution can effectively guarantee the one-hundred-percent-secure keeping of any collectible. But worrying won't work either. Mark it, record it, secure and insure it, and relax.

CHAPTER X

A Checklist for Collectors

Before you buy any item for your collection, you should always determine whether that item would be an asset or a liability. To help you in making that decision, here is a checklist of some of the most common (as well as a few not-so-common) factors to consider *before* you buy. Keep in mind that this checklist is a general one and can be used for everything from coins to costumes.

☐ 1. Can you tell if the item is genuine?

☐ 2. If the item is genuine, is it of the quality that the seller says it is?

☐ 3. Does the item have noticeable (or even hidden) flaws or imperfections?

☐ 4. What type of documentation is available for the item? Is this a satisfactory guarantee to you of its worth?

☐ 5. Does it have beauty?

☐ 6. How much artistic value does the item possess?

☐ 7. Does the piece have a particular attraction for you? Are you absolutely captivated by it?

☐ 8. What connection does the item have with your family background or nationality?

☐ 9. Is your interest in the item based primarily on the interests of others?

☐ 10. How different is this product from its related items? Is it of a higher or lesser quality?

☐ 11. How intricate was the work involved in creating the item?

☐ 12. Did the work require a lot of skill or just a little?

☐ 13. Is this a one-time opportunity that you must take advantage of now?

☐ 14. Do you know enough about the item to be able to make a sound decision about it?

☐ 15. If not, how long will you need to collect more information?

☐ 16. From where will you be able to obtain more information about the item?

☐ 17. Does the item have value in and of itself? In other words, are the materials used valuable?

☐ 18. How much does the item cost to make? Is the price much higher than that?

☐ 19. Are there other factors besides the cost of materials and labor that could account for a high price?

☐ 20. What are these other factors: age, scarcity, quality?

☐ 21. Will the item be a good gift or a valuable heirloom for generations to come?

☐ 22. What is the historical significance of the item?

☐ 23. How easy is it to produce a facsimile? Could you tell the difference between an authentic and an artificial one?

☐ 24. Was the item once the property of a famous person, or was it used during some great historical event?

☐ 25. How much popularity does the item have now? Is it popular with only a select group of people or with collectors?

☐ 26. What is the projected popularity of the item in the future? Will it increase, decrease, or always be pretty much the same? (Note that some items, like antiques, while they never reach the high peak of other, more faddish products, maintain constant value in the marketplace.)

☐ 27. Does the item require special protection, insurance, or refinishing in order to maintain its value?

☐ 28. Is the item part of a set? If I buy it separately, will that decrease its value?

☐ 29. How easily can I sell this item?

☐ 30. Is this something practically anyone would buy, or must I find a dealer or auctioneer to buy it back?

☐ 31. How much money could I expect to make if I sell this item?

☐ 32. Is the profit I would make equal to the money I would have to spend in refinishing, storing, or transporting the item?

☐ 33. How many other items of this type (approximately) are available? Is supply greater than demand?

☐ 34. Do you know the seller personally? If not, what guarantees do you have of the seller's reliability and/or expertise?

☐ 35. Why do you want the item (other than for financial profit)?

☐ 36. Are your reasons for buying the item sound?

☐ 37. Finally, is the item worth all the time and money you will spend on it?

CHAPTER XI

Buying and Selling

It's happened. You've arrived at a level of some expertise in your field. You've reached the point where you know what you want. You have a good idea of approximately how much your collectibles sell for on the current retail market.

One thing to keep in the back of your mind as you purchase or sell any item, however, is that its true value is not always equivalent to its catalog price. With many collectibles —especially antiques and works of art—prices paid often depend more on buyer-seller wheeling and dealing than on any reliable price guide. This may mean that you are able to obtain a piece for less than its current value in price guides. But, more often, it means that the dealer, experienced in bargaining, will get more than that catalog list price. In short, the price you pay or receive is more a result of individual bargaining than of standard prices.

With this in mind, how can you get the best price when you buy or sell? Let's take buying first.

Buying from Dealers and Collectors

Even before you approach a dealer, private collector, or other source of an item you want, you should have a general knowledge of an upper and lower price range for your particular item. In addition, you should also check your own financial situation thoroughly to determine the maximum amount you can reasonably spend on the item or items you want to buy. This will be based not only on the money you have to spend, but also on how valuable you consider the item.

Then, when you are ready to approach a seller, follow these guidelines:

1. Don't expect a bargain. If you do, you are likely to be disappointed.

2. Don't waste too much time looking over items other than the one that interests you. Get a general idea of the seller's prices, but don't ask the price of everything in the store. This will only irritate the seller.

3. Don't accept the line that the price of everything is going up. This is not always true.

4. When you offer prices, start with bids lower than your maximum amount.

5. Look at the item carefully before you buy and do not hesitate to point out any major flaws. They could lower the price. (Do not nitpick, however, as this can make the seller unwilling to cooperate.)

6. Avoid an attitude of either naïveté or omniscience. Neither will help you secure a bargain.

7. It may help to buy a not-too-valuable item at the price the dealer requests; this will establish your relationship as a customer.

8. Don't let the whole store know your intentions. Almost any dealer will respect you more if you keep your voice down.

9. Always display a take-it-or-leave-it attitude to any item under negotiation. That is, don't make the dealer think you want it so badly that you're willing to pay just about any price to have it.

10. If the dealer is handling someone else's merchandise, ask to have the owner contacted about your offer.

11. Remember that the wholesale/retail factor applies to any merchandise you exchange with a dealer. This means that you sell wholesale and buy retail. Unless you see a great advantage to the item the dealer has, it is wise to avoid barter.

12. The best times to buy are in January (a poor month for sales) and before the dealer goes on vacation.

13. After you have settled on a price, ask the dealer for terms of credit. This is especially useful if you really feel an item is valuable but don't have the cash on hand to purchase it.

14. If you do pay in cash, ask for a discount. Dealers will often give it, just for the advantage of having sure, ready money.

15. If you're buying in a foreign country, beware of anyone trying to take advantage of your lack of knowledge of the market in that country.

16. A retail registration number, a business card, and/or a sense of expertise will often get you a special dealer's discount rate. If it's offered to you, take it.

17. Pay no attention to the dealer's high-pressure tactics; and, for your own sake, don't give the dealer a rundown of all the pieces you've bought and sold.

18. Don't offer an unreasonably low price; this will only discourage any further negotiations.

Buying at Auction

Auctions are the collector's joy—and nightmare. It is unquestionably true that auctions bring together huge quantities of collectibles. Yet the social, psychological, time, and business pressures often work against finding a value. The rules of looking for future finds discussed in this book should be followed at auctions as well. Here's a list of special tips to being a wise bidder.

1. *Know your limit*

We all know the fellow who went to the race track and said, "I'll gamble until I lose fifty dollars, and then I quit." All too often he quits only after he's lost every cent he has.

The same frenzy holds true at auctions. Perfectly knowledgeable collectors will somehow get caught up in the auction aura. When the bidding is fast and furious, it's easy to get carried away by the excitement of the moment and bid more than an item is worth or more than you were planning to pay.

The solution is to write next to each item the *maximum* you'll pay. This writing exercise is done before the sale while you are calm and objective. Do not budge from this price under any circumstances.

2. *Know the item*

You must visit the auction before the sale begins and carefully examine each item. The mechanical coin bank that may look fine from a distance might upon close examination, turn out to be (*a*) a reproduction, (*b*) repainted, or (*c*) not working—or all of the above. Pay careful attention to the qualities, condition, and workmanship, and let your own judgment guide you on an item's merits. Don't trust catalog descriptions or others' comments. Be sure you bid only on the exact item you have seen in the auction exhibit.

3. *Attending the auction*

If you're looking for future collectibles, Sotheby Parke Bernet is not for you. Tomorrow's collectibles, at affordable prices, are located in out-of-the-way places. Rainy and snowy days bring out the smallest number of bidders.

Bargains are harder to find than ever before. Not only are you competing with dealers, but with inflation-wary investors as well. A recent front-page newspaper story

(*New York Times*, page 1, February 3, 1979) talks of the rush to "coins, stamps, violins, old tools, antiques, art, model trains, . . . anything that will appreciate faster than the dollar shrinks."

Find out which auctions in your area are the best for collectibles. Before bidding the first time, observe a few bidding sessions and make sure they will accept your personal check or that you have sufficient cash. If, when you are bidding, you think someone else's bid is suspicious (e.g., an owner is bidding to raise the price), ask the bidder to be identified. This is legal. If the bidder refuses to be identified, withdraw from the auction.

4. Learn auction language

At some sales, bidding is in one-dollar increments, while at others it's in twenty-five-dollar increments. Find out which is the case before you discover that your hand in the air bought you a Coke tray for $50, not $2.

In addition, auctioneers often use language such as "it could be" or "looks like" to describe an item. A "Wedgwood-type" plate is definitely not Wedgwood.

Auctions hold a world of fun and collectibles. But know and investigate before you buy.

General Tips for Selling

Before you go about trying to find someone to buy your entire collection or an item in your collection, you must know when to sell. Part of your decision will be based on the current market. If prices are higher than those you paid, you will probably be able to sell at a profit.

Generally, when it comes time to sell, you are much better off if you have had some experience in selling while you have been forming your collection. For one thing, dealers will know you; for another, you'll probably be more familiar with the ins and outs of your particular market.

Thus, the first piece of advice about selling is to get involved in it before you absolutely have to. This will give you a fairly good idea of where you have to go to get the best prices, when to sell, how long it takes to negotiate a sale, and what selling tactics work best for you.

Beyond this, have your collection appraised, both by individual items and as a whole, by an expert who is not interested in purchasing. This will give you an indication (an updated one, if you have had it appraised before) of what you can expect to receive for it. Naturally, you should never allow the collection to go for a price much lower than the appraiser's estimate.

If you have items in your collection that are not as valuable (or ones that are not proven genuine), sell them separately. Otherwise, they may decrease the value of the collection as a whole.

Check up on your insurance before you sell. Are the items protected against loss due to transportation, breakage, et cetera? Also, make sure your inventory of the collection is complete. You're much better off if you have a complete record of everything, both before and after you sell.

Selling at Auction

To determine whether or not you should sell at a particular auction, you should check it out carefully. It helps if you have bought items from that auction house in the past. The proprietors will thus recognize and be more willing to cooperate with you. Any auction house whose reputation is questionable should be avoided.

One factor that strongly determines whether to sell at auction is the specific collection you are selling. You may have a collection, or pieces of a collection, that could be combined with others' collections to form an exciting, highly profitable sale of oriental porcelain, for example. On the other hand, your pieces may be much more valuable than others being auctioned. Before entering your pieces in an auction, know what else is being bid for.

Once you have determined that you want to enter your pieces in a particular auction, you'll have to settle the terms with the auctioneer in charge. Generally, you'll receive no more than 75 percent of the price bid for any item or collection of items. But how much the auctioneer charges varies with each auction house. When business is slow, or when the auctioneer is offered an exceptional collection, you're likely to receive a better price.

Included in the arrangements you make with the auctioneer should be who pays for the expenses involved (transportation, display, insurance, photos, packing, catalog, repairs, the exact amount needed for these expenses, and the terms of payment.

You should also establish a base price (the minimum amount you will accept as a bid) for each item or the collection as a whole. This should be in writing, as should any other agreement you make with the auctioneer. In fact, it is wise to have a lawyer draw up a contract between you and the auctioneer and make sure the auctioneer is the one responsible for paying you. Unless the auction would be prohibitively expensive otherwise, the sale should not take place in your home. This only increases your aggravation. One last note: If at all possible, you should attend the auction!

Selling to Dealers

As has been mentioned, the first thing to remember when selling to dealers is that they're buying wholesale with the intention of selling retail. This automatically puts you at a disadvantage from the start.

Generally, any dealer will not pay much more than half the price expected from the resale of an item. In fact, most dealers will start by asking you what you want for the item; if your offer is lower than they expected, they'll jump at the chance. To prevent this, throw the question back at them. Let them quote the first price. (Again, remember to have a disinterested appraiser evaluate your merchandise so you have a good idea what it's worth.) Don't accept the first offer you receive unless and until you check out alternative offers. And don't accept any offer that is not advantageous to you.

Some dealers will offer an outrageously high price for parts of a collection, in the hope that you will let the rest of it go for far below market value. Don't fall for this trick. If the buyer makes a highly technical or complicated offer, check it out with your lawyer before you agree to it.

Never give out your address until you are aware of the potential buyer's qualifications. This will put you at a disadvantage. And don't put any money into redoing any part of your collection; let the dealer do that, since you will not be paid for any repairs or refinishing.

Guidelines for Bargaining with Dealers
When Selling Your Items

1. Understand the economic reality of the situation. The dealer is not going to be able to sell your piece for the same price he gives you. Expect to receive less than the dealer's listed price.

2. Don't ask the dealer how much he would pay for every item in your collection; stick with only one or two at a time. (You may, however, offer one item at a discount if the dealer agrees to buy another item at a higher price.)

3. Don't be fooled by the dealer's argument that he can only offer low prices because of high overhead costs.

4. When offering a piece for sale, start with high prices and work your way down from there.

5. Know the value of your item and be willing to defend it against dealer criticisms.

6. Establish yourself as a customer before you attempt to sell anything to a dealer.

7. The same respect for privacy applies as much to

selling as to buying. Don't let your negotiations be heard by everyone nearby.

8. Consult several dealers before you finalize a sale.

9. If a dealer offers you an extremely high price, beware. He may be trying to con you into thinking he'll always give you the best deals.

10. The best times to sell are those times when the dealer is trying to increase his stock: immediately after vacation, early spring, and right before Christmas.

11. Unless you have dealt with a particular dealer for a long time, it's wise to accept only cash for your items.

Other Sources of Sales

Auctions and dealers are not the only places where you can sell your collection. For more valuable collections, a museum might be the place. Another increasingly profitable source of sales is large corporations. To enhance their image, many corporations are building collections of works of art, jewelry, and other valuables. If your items interest them, they just might buy. For the not-so-valuable collection, flea markets are a good source of revenue. Or you may want to open your own shop, if you have enough merchandise to make it worthwhile. In addition, many collecting periodicals and newspapers offer their readers a classified section, through which items can be sold.

No matter where you eventually sell your collection, the important thing to remember is to look for the best price.

CHAPTER XII

The Ten Commandments of Collecting

1. *Thou shalt not buy anything without being absolutely positive that it is genuine.*

    Too much has been sold over the years that turned out to be phony, ersatz, fake, bogus, and untrue. Don't wake up one morning to the awful discovery that you once had a $30,000 collection of genuine Tiffany glass that isn't genuine and is really worth a mere $250.

2. *Thou shalt not believe in miracles.*

    When you happened to see a real Dali print in a small out-of-the-way store, and the owner of the store doesn't seem to realize that it's a signed Dali, and you think you're making some kind of killing—*beware!* You are not making a killing. In all probability, you are the one who is getting ripped off.

3. *Thou shalt not buy mass-produced collectibles.*

    Too many people, over the past two decades, have been convinced that they are getting a truly rare item when they buy anything that's labeled "limited edition." These so-called limited editions are really limited only to about twenty-five million copies. There is no limit unless a specific number is given and unless a master mold is broken in a public ceremony.

4. Thou shalt not buy unless thou art certain that thou can also sell.

You must know if there is a market for something. If you are totally positive that you will be able to resell the collectible you are considering, then make that purchase. But if you are involved in some vague speculation, or if something just looks like a good deal, you're better off staying away.

5. When in doubt, thou shalt buy American.

Remember this axiom: The closer to home you are, the safer you will be. That's why American collectibles have the popularity today, far more than any foreign products. American coins are more in demand than foreign coins. American art is more popular than foreign art. American goods are more popular, by and large, than foreign-made goods. This popularity is also a form of insurance. As long as more Americans continue to get involved in collectibles, then the price of American collectibles will rise higher and higher.

6. Thou shalt not rely on just one opinion.

Let's say that Fritz Schmidlap, the world's greatest living expert on Walt Disney collectibles, has stated with total assurance, "The value of the Mickey Mouse soap dish will triple in the next twelve months."

Only one problem: Fritz Schmidlap doesn't know what he's talking about. And the fact that he's self-advertised as "the greatest expert" on something doesn't make it true.

When in doubt, the safest course of action is to get several opinions.

7. Thou shalt not follow the fads.

Last year it was Tiffany. Lamps that once sold for $25 were selling for $500. Then the bottom fell out of the market and they were selling for $25 again. The year before it was Centennial collectibles. Items that were selling for $100 suddenly tripled in value. Then (after the end of the American Bicentennial, naturally!) the bottom fell out of that market. Next year it's going to be Olympic memorabilia. But you can be sure of this: Prices that go up too fast will also go down too fast.

The moral: The best way to invest in anything is to be certain that there is a steady and continuous market for buyers and sellers. If something is a fad, you could be heading for a lot of trouble.

8. *Thou shalt specialize.*

Don't attempt to become totally knowledgeable about every area of collectibles. Focus your interest in a narrow area and get to know that thoroughly.

Once you have decided on which area you want to pursue, get to know every aspect of it. Follow the auctions, read the books, get any special newsletters that are published in these areas. And, most important, get to know other people who have the same interests.

9. *Thou shalt keep thy collection in good order.*

Keep a record of all receipts so you know how much you paid for something. Keep your collection in good order, well marked, well organized, and safe. (And try not to boast of the value of your collection to people you don't really know. That's the best way to invite a thief into your home.)

10. *Most important: Thou shalt enjoy thy collection.*

Remember this: Your collection is for enjoyment, for fun. Unless you are getting pleasure from collecting, stop whatever you are doing and try something else. Collecting should be a joy and not a chore.

Part Two: A Catalog of Collectibles

Introduction

This part of the book will provide an introduction to a wide range of collectibles. The word "introduction" has been chosen with care. All a general text such as this can do is provide the basic facts and some background to help you choose possible areas of collection. Once you've chosen ones that interest you, study them in more detail before investing significant sums. Careless selection and investment are not likely to lead to the profits you want.

Investment charts are provided to give a "general" idea of price ranges. Do not use these prices for buying or selling; use them only as guidelines. Prices can vary a great deal depending on market conditions and on the collectible's physical condition which may affect the value of an item by as much as 1,000 percent.

Moreover, as you gain more experience and expertise in collecting, you will be better able to distinguish the genuine collector's item from the faked or mass-produced one. The seasoned collector, for instance, would know that most Kennedy autographs are the result of his famous signature machine, and would be able to spot the *genuine* autographs, the only ones that have any value.

Investment charts have not been included for some categories for one of two reasons: either more specific knowledge is needed to determine price, or the collection's saleability is heavily dependent upon demand. It is impossible, for example, to price stained glass in a book like this. A four-foot-square piece of glass could sell for $50 or $5,000. My general advice would be to invest only small amounts in this category until you feel confident in your ability to judge value. A collection of matchbook covers is an example of a collectible category that could be almost worthless unless you find a specialized collector.

Welcome to the world of tomorrow's collectibles. Among the categories that follow, there is sure to be one that will set you on the road to collecting success.

A Catalog of Collectibles

Advertising Memorabilia

If you look in your pocket and find a ball-point pen, there is a good chance it has an advertising message on it. The advertising specialty industry will top two billion dollars this year. With advertising as much a part of American life as baseball, television, and automobiles, it should come as no surprise that advertising collecting has a future.

Since advertising giveaways were traditionally viewed as worthless, many of the historical pieces are now in short supply. Those existing were seldom treated with care and are therefore usually in poor condition.

Although all giveaways have an interest level, the most enthusiasm is for early editions of popular manufacturers. Coca-Cola is an obvious example, but also watch for items from such majors as Borden's, Wrigley, Nabisco and Procter & Gamble. Early radio premiums (Tom Mix rings, Little Orphan Annie cups) are also in big demand.

You can assume that current premiums will be sought after, too. Just a few years ago Exxon (then Esso) distributed free "Put a Tiger in Your Tank" mugs that already bring $2 and more at flea markets. Start saving anything with a brand name such as glasses, letter openers, and even supermarket game tickets. Americans will continue to love advertising items, causing them to rise in value.

Just about anything can and has been used to promote a

company's products. Below are just a few of the items created
for the express purpose of advertising.

ITEM	DATE	DESCRIPTION	CURRENT VALUE
Thermometers	early 20th century	Advertising anything from root beer to alfalfa seed	$4.00–$17.50
Coca-Cola trays	1899–1920	Various designs	$100–$1,000
Coca-Cola bookmark	1904	Picture of Lillian Russell	$50
Match safes	late 18th, early 19th centuries	Lettered or pictured; some gold- or silver-plated	$8.50–$38.00
Paperweights	late 18th, early 19th centuries	In cast iron, steel, brass, and glass	$3.75–$65.00
Mirrors	late 18th, early 19th centuries	Any and all kinds; most famous one advertises Buster Brown shoes	$6.60–$25.00
Trays	late 18th, early 19th centuries	Advertising everything from soup to beer to ham	$10–$50
Moxie mobile	1920s	Tin car used to advertise Moxie beverage	up to $250
Old catalogs	early 1900s	Everything from Milton Bradley's School Aids catalog to Barnum's Iron & Wire Works catalog	$5–$18

Autographs

To obtain a fabulous collection certain to be worthwhile in future years all one needs is a collection of postage stamps and a package of notepaper. Tomorrow's costly autographs are a few letters away.

The hobby of autograph collecting is just starting a new boom period. Like stamp collecting this hobby offers a look into history, yet is even more exciting because it provides personal and private insights into the past. Most of today's autograph collectors started when they stood outside a stadium locker room and obtained the signature of some exciting ball player. Additions came when a famous person was seen in a restaurant and could be badgered into signing a napkin or the back of a menu.

First let us clear up some of the myths. Sports figures and show business personalities have the least interest among real collectors and the least chance of appreciation in value. The first problem is that they are very plentiful and the second is that they are often not authentic. One Hollywood star admits to having no less than a dozen secretaries schooled in signing autographed pictures. And the invention of the automatic handwriting machine makes even seemingly personal notes questionable.

The best autographs are those connected to real communications that deal with an important issue. So, for example, a letter from one military man to another explaining an issue of war will often fetch a higher price than a president's signature on a matchbook cover.

Surprisingly, many famous people still answer much of their own mail. I have seen handwritten notes from playwrights, politicians, business tycoons, and inventors who replied to a ten-year-old boy's inquiries about facets of their work. Building up a collection today for success tomorrow can often be accomplished with little money but much imagination. A sincere letter with a self-addressed envelope will often bring a reply from a best-selling novelist who is the folk hero of the future.

Autographs go in and out of fashion. Currently war heroes and musicians are sought after. But again, the contents of a letter add much to the value of an autograph.

Current prices range widely. Here are some recent retail prices:

AUTOGRAPH	CURRENT PRICE
P. T. Barnum	$ 25
Button Gwinnett	$65,000
Ernest Hemingway	$ 100
John F. Kennedy	$ 1,000
Henry Wadsworth Longfellow	$ 20
Mozart	$25,000
Adelina Patti	$ 50
Rudolph Valentino	$ 150
Orville Wright	$ 100

(It is important to understand that the value varies widely with the type of letter or document that precedes the signature)

Although the future looks bright for old autographs, the real profits will be made by starting a collection from scratch with people you can reach by mail.

Banks

In the remains of early civilizations small earthenware containers were found which we now know were the first banks. For the collector, however, the real interest is in the so-called mechanical money boxes. A combination of levers and springs causes the coin to be deposited following some action by a portion of the bank. A typical contraption is one in which a coin is placed in the hand of a cast-iron figure, the weight of the coin causing the hand to drop it through an opened trap-door in the base of the bank.

Mechanical banks were popular from 1880 to 1940.

Literally thousands of variations were produced. Originals of early cast-iron banks can bring $10,000 and more in Americana auctions. Probably the best known manufacturer is J. & A. Stevens of Cromwell, Connecticut. The Stevens name is stamped right onto the bank.

A search through flea markets will sometimes uncover these charming toys. Here again the buyer needs to be careful of mass-produced items that are sometimes represented as originals. Most reproductions have badly joined parts and always appear freshly painted, no matter how skillful the forger.

This is an obvious growth area. Only mechanical banks have real potential for growth. Simple still, or nonmechanical, banks seem to hold little interest with the collecting community.

Books—Old and New

Books are timeless transports to any destination in any era. Fact or fiction, poetry or prose, books convey the permanent word to many generations of readers. Additionally, books are an alternative to traditional investments. Unlike stocks, books provide tangible pleasure as well as profit. Book prices will appreciate steadily, at a relatively stable rate. Finally, there are a variety of books that can be profitably collected.

The earliest books, incunabula, are still relatively inexpensive to collect. True antiques, incunabula (literally translated as "imitation manuscripts") are printed mostly in Latin and are collected more for profit than pleasure.

The total factual information in print on United States history includes memoirs, diaries, autobiographies, and some illustrated books. All of these have strong collection interest.

Illustrated books are noted for their artwork, as well as for their typography, paper material, and decorative bindings. Often private press and children's books are illustrated. These books may be collected for profit as well as pleasure. Books with hand-colored engravings and actual photographs are especially valuable.

Limited- and first-edition books are most often collected for profit. By their nature, they create an artificial rarity that escalates their value. If you're not sure if you have a first edition, ask the publisher when the book was first published. Usually the first editions have only one date on the copyright page.

The following is a sample list of books for your collecting profit and pleasure.

COLLECTIBLE BOOKS: FIRST EDITIONS AND CONTEMPORARY FIRST EDITIONS

AUTHOR	TITLE	PLACE AND DATE OF PUBLICATION	DESCRIPTION & CLASSIFICATION	CURRENT VALUE
Albee, Edward	*Who's Afraid of Virginia Woolf?*	New York, 1962	First edition Contemporary Fine condition	$35
Alcott, Louisa May	*Little Women* (Part One)	Boston, 1868	First edition Mint condition Does not say "Part One" on spine	$800– $1,200
Barthelme, Donald	*Come Back, Dr. Caligari*	Boston, 1964	First edition Contemporary Fine condition	$25
Bradbury, Ray	*Dark Carnival*	Sauk City, 1947	First edition Contemporary Fine condition	$100
Burroughs, William	*Port of Saints*	London, 1973	First condition Contemporary Signed/200 copies Fine condition	$50

COLLECTIBLE BOOKS: FIRST EDITIONS AND CONTEMPORARY FIRST EDITIONS (Continued)

AUTHOR	TITLE	PLACE AND DATE OF PUBLICATION	DESCRIPTION & CLASSIFICATION	CURRENT VALUE
Cather, Willa	The Troll Garden	New York, 1905	First Edition Mint condition Lists McClure & Co. on spine	$100– $150
Dahlberg, Edward	Bottom Dogs	London, 1929	First edition Contemporary 520 copies Fine condition	$85
Didion, Joan	Play It as It Lays	New York, 1970	First edition Contemporary Fine condition	$25
Emerson, Ralph Waldo	May-Day and Other Pieces	Boston, 1867	First edition Mint condition Error on page 184— "flowers" for "hours"	$75– $100

Author	Title	Place, Date	Condition	Price
Farrell, James	*No Star is Lost*	New York, 1938	First edition Contemporary Fine condition	$45
Frost, Robert	*A Boy's Will*	London, 1913	First edition Mint condition Bound in brown or bronze pebbled cloth	$950–$1,150
Gordon, Caroline	*Aleck Maury, Sportsman*	New York, 1934	First edition Contemporary Fine condition	$65
Greene, Graham	*The Man Within*	London, 1929	First edition Contemporary Fine condition	$100
Hawkes, John	*The Beetle Leg*	New York, 1951	First edition Contemporary Fine condition	$25
Kinnell, Galway	*Bitter Victory*	Garden City, 1956	First edition Contemporary Fine condition	$25

COLLECTIBLE BOOKS: FIRST EDITIONS AND CONTEMPORARY FIRST EDITIONS (Continued)

AUTHOR	TITLE	PLACE AND DATE OF PUBLICATION	DESCRIPTION & CLASSIFICATION	CURRENT VALUE
Lardner, Ring W.	What of It!	New York, 1925	First edition Mint condition Pages numbered 19, 201, 200 (with dust jacket)	$75
Levertov, Denise	Overland to the Islands	North Carolina, 1958	First edition Contemporary Inscribed Fine condition	$65
McClure, Michael	The Beard	Berkeley, 1965	First edition Contemporary 350 copies Fine condition	$65
MacDiarmid, Hugh	Poems to Paintings by William Johnstone		First edition Contemporary Signed/100 copies Fine condition	$20

Merwin. W. S.	*The Dancing Bears*	New Haven, 1954	First edition Contemporary Fine condition	$25
Miller, Henry	*Plexus*	Paris, 1952 two volumes	First edition Contemporary Fine condition	$150
Murdoch, Iris	*The Bell*	London, 1958	First edition Contemporary Fine condition	$25
Nemerov, Howard	*The Image and The Law*	New York, 1947	First edition Contemporary Fine condition	$45
Percy, Walker	*The Moviegoer*	New York, 1961	First edition Contemporary Fine condition	$25
Poe, Edgar Allan	*Poems*	New York, 1831	First edition Mint condition Marked "Second Edition" on title page Rare	$10,000

COLLECTIBLE BOOKS: FIRST EDITIONS AND CONTEMPORARY FIRST EDITIONS (Continued)

AUTHOR	TITLE	PLACE AND DATE OF PUBLICATION	DESCRIPTION & CLASSIFICATION	CURRENT VALUE
Queen, Ellery	The Chinese Orange Mystery	New York, 1934	First edition Contemporary Fine condition	$30
Roth, Phillip	Goodbye, Columbus	Boston, 1959	First edition Contemporary Fine condition	$40
Stafford, William	That Other Alone	Wisconsin, 1973	First condition Contemporary Signed/120 copies Fine condition	$40
Updike, John	The Angels	Pensacola, 1968	First edition Contemporary Signed/150 copies Fine condition	$60
Wolfe, Thomas	Look Homeward, Angel	New York, 1929	First edition Mint condition Scribner seal on copyright page, Wolfe's picture on jacket	$200–$400

Welty, Eudora	A Curtain of Green	New York, 1941	First edition Contemporary Fine condition	$85
Wright, James	The Green Wall	Connecticut, 1957	First edition Contemporary Fine condition	$30

ILLUSTRATED AND AMERICANA BOOKS

Atherton, Gertrude	The Gorgeous Isle	New York, 1908	First edition Delicate illustrations by Coles Phillips, bound in Chinese red cloth	$50
DeVoto, Bernard	Across the Wide Missouri	Boston, 1947	First edition Americana Fine condition, with dust jacket	$125

COLLECTIBLE BOOKS: FIRST EDITIONS AND CONTEMPORARY FIRST EDITIONS (Continued)

AUTHOR	TITLE	PLACE AND DATE OF PUBLICATION	DESCRIPTION & CLASSIFICATION	CURRENT VALUE
Gregg, Josiah	Commerce of the Prairies	New York, 1884	First edition Americana Fine condition	$300
Helper, Hinton	The Land of Gold	Baltimore, 1885	First edition Americana Fine condition	$125
Remington, Frederic	Done in the Open	New York, 1902	First edition Classic drawings with matching rhymes	$150
Smith, John	The General History of Virginia, New England and Summer Isles	1627	First edition Mint condition	$11,640
Zenas, Leonard	Narrative		First edition Extremely rare	$15,000

PRIVATE PRESS BOOKS

AUTHOR	TITLE	PLACE AND DATE OF PUBLICATION	DESCRIPTION & CLASSIFICATION	CURRENT VALUE
Dickens, Charles	Collected Works	Not available	Limited edition Nonesuch Press (23-volume set)	$2,350
Ruskin, John	The Nature of Gothic	Not available	Limited edition Kelmscott Press	$450–$550
Shelley, Percy	Selected Poems	Not available	Limited edition Doves Press	$500

Bottles—The King of the Collectibles

Bottles, combined with paper cartons and tin cans, account for an estimated 95 percent of today's supermarket packaging. Most are manufactured in such profusion that, when empty, they contribute noticeably to a growing ecology crisis, yet some are rare and have been made in limited editions.

In 1964 the James B. Beam Distilling Company issued a commemorative ceramic whiskey bottle in the shape of the First National Bank of Chicago. Distributed in small numbers, this bottle sold for as much as $2,000.

Such bottles are scarce. With prices varying inversely as to availability, most limited-edition and figural bottles may be purchased for as little as $3.95.

Bottles are colorful collectibles for decorative, rather than profitable, pleasure. Despite the abundance, bottles are, for the most part, often only a dust collector's dream. However, as one can see from the chart that follows, their value varies widely. The future appreciation depends on the type of bottle, not on the category.

BOTTLES

COMPANY	DESCRIPTION	CIRCULATION	ORIGINAL COST	CURRENT VALUE
Pictorial Bottle Review Magazine Series	Gold, commemorative bottles in shapes of a gold camel, an antique peddler and a wrangler	Series of 3 1970–72 1,000–1,200	$17.95–$29.95	Not available
Collector's Art Limited Bottle Series	Porcelain bottles in the shapes of birds and animals	Series of 3 1970, 1972 1,200	$10.95	$17–$20
James B. Beam Distilling Co.	Commemorative whiskey bottles	Series of 8 1964–69 Not available	$10–$18	$11–$2,000
D. J. W. Dant Co.	Figural bottles in white milk glass	Series of 2 1969 Not available	$6–$8	$8–$17
Ezra Brooks Distilling Co.	Figural bottles	Series of 4 1968–70 Not available	$5–$40	$10–$120
Lionstone Distilleries, Ltd.	Bottles, portraying Old West characters	Series of 4 1969 Not available	$5–$20	$20–$28
Wheaton Glass Co.	Hand-blown and pressed glass decanters	Series of 4 Not available	$10	$7–$48
Eggerman Type-Weil	Bohemian designs engraved on red crystal decanters	Series of 4 1970–73 50–500	$35–$45	$45–$97

Clothing

Though old clothing is unlikely to appreciate in value, there is investment potential in so-called celebrity clothing.

When people buy celebrity clothing they are buying on the principle of reflected glory, believing that a mundane garment is valuable simply because it touched a favored star. As an investment, celebrity clothing offers possibilities, but a good deal of care needs to be exercised. The obvious pitfall is proving authenticity. For example, a recent advertisement offered the T-shirt of a famous rock star cut into one-inch squares. The promoter announced that he had sold over three thousand squares. Simple arithmetic would tell you that the rock star could not possibly wear a T-shirt that large. Even when the source is reputable, one questions the sincerity of the celebrity. One television star reports receiving weekly requests from charity auctions to feature some article of his clothing. To fill these requests, he buys ties by the dozens, throws them around his neck for a moment, and sends them with a seemingly personally typed note that begins, "Enclosed is a tie I recently wore. . . ."

If you are a clothes fancier, however, this could make a perfect hobby. Queen Victoria's clothes (right down to her underwear) appear regularly in London auctions. More recently, movie-star wardrobe mistresses earned fantastic sums by offering outfits designed for Hollywood heart-breakers.

The secret to making this hobby profitable is to obtain some sort of document that assures it is authentic. The fact that John Wayne wore a red bandanna in the movie hardly proves that yours is the actual red bandanna. Letters signed by the celebrity are all-important. The future potential for Frank Sinatra's shirt, Jimmy Carter's robe, or Walter Cronkite's handkerchief are at best clouded, but if you buy an item cheaply enough and can document its original owner, you may have a fine investment.

As for clothes in general, stick with intrinsically expensive pieces such as furs, fine silks, or detailed garments with much handwork.

Coins for Collectors

In 1792 the United States established its own mint in Philadelphia. The dollar was designated as a standard unit of commerce and a decimal system was adopted. Early coins emphasized the value concept and were minted so that a copper cent would contain a cent's worth of copper.

It was not until the 1850s that the business of coin collecting began to evolve. "Business strikes" (minting of coins for the sole purpose of conducting commercial transactions) were minted for commercial use, as always. But it wasn't until 1858 that the first collector's "proof set" was offered for sale to the general public. Proof sets (made for presentation) have a mirrorlike finish and are sold for more than the metal value in the coin. Special collectors' sets may also be minted in platinum or aluminum. Most other coins are minted in copper, nickel, or silver.

Gold coins are the highest-valued coins minted. They represent the most desired metal and are made in convenient and artistic forms.

Coins are easy to collect, buy, and sell. They require simple storage and handling precautions and are a strong, steady investment for the commercial collector.

UNITED STATES COINS

YEAR ISSUED	DENOMINATION	DESCRIPTION	ESTIMATED CURRENT VALUE
1910	Nickel	A proof set "liberty head" coin "CENTS" indicated	$55
1795	Half dime	Uncirculated Marked by "flowing hair"	$1,100
1832	Half dime	Uncirculated Marked by "capped bust"	$148
1862	Half dime	A proof set "Liberty" seated	$96
1837	Dime	Uncirculated Also known as the "no stars" dime	$623
1874	Dime	Uncirculated An arrow indicates date position	$220
1876	Twenty-cent piece	Proof set Only one type issued	$90
1818	Quarter	Proof set Features the "capped bust" and large typed letters	$990
1861	Quarter	Proof set	$205
1878	Quarter	Proof set	$180
1917	Type-1 quarter	Uncirculated "Liberty" standing	$80
1805	Half-dollar	Uncirculated Features a "draped bust" on one side, the small eagle on the reverse side	$875
1844	Half-dollar	Uncirculated No motto "Liberty" seated	$175
1874	Half-dollar	Uncirculated Arrows at the date	$360

1886	Half-dollar	Uncirculated With motto "Liberty" seated	$240
1942	Half-dollar	Proof set "Liberty" walking	$60
1863	Silver dollar	Uncirculated "Liberty" seated No motto	$340
1895	Silver dollar	Proof Morgan set	$5,850

UNITED STATES GOLD COINS

YEAR ISSUED	DENOMINATION	DESCRIPTION	ESTIMATED CURRENT VALUE
1855	Gold dollar	Uncirculated Very scarce	$1,490
1831	Two-and-a-half-dollar piece	Uncirculated With "Liberty" head	$1,900
1879	Four-dollar piece	Proof set Marked by "flowing hair"	$9,870
1835	Five-dollar piece	Uncirculated Indian type	$485
1911	Ten-dollar piece	Uncirculated Indian-head type	$4,400
1928	Twenty-dollar piece	Uncirculated Marked by Saint Gaudens	$165

Comic Books

In the thirties and forties, children could buy their comic books for ten cents. No more: Today, those same comic books may be worth up to $300 *each*. That's a greater increase, percentagewise, than just about any other collectible. Yet, amazingly, many people continue to just throw them away. With a little digging in attics, closets, old drawers, flea markets, and household sales, you might find that Superman, Batman, Archie, and other heroes could give you a good supply of petty cash.

Of special value are the following comics series.

TITLE	DATE	CURRENT PRICE
Detective Comics (introduction of Batman)	May 1939	up to $3,000
Four Color Comics of Disney Characters (Dell Publications)	1942	up to $1,000
Action Comics #1 (introduction of Superman)	1938	up to $5,000
Red Raven #1 (only issue of this comics series)	Unknown	up to $800
Marvel Comics #1 (only issue with this title)	Unknown	up to $6,000

Condition is of great importance. As a general rule the more popular characters (Disney, Batman, Superman) offer the greatest opportunity for growth. War comics have received some recent interest and speculation.

Depression Glass

Depression glass is a term used to describe the popular, decorative, man-made tableware most often used from 1920 to 1940. It was characterized by a machine-molded design and by bright colors frequently used to camouflage bubbles and flaws in the glass. It was manufactured in geometric, flashy shapes and simple Art Deco forms. Patterns were floral or traditional. Many patterns employed optical illusions for additional appeal.

Depression glass was very inexpensive. During the Great Depression years, separate pieces cost as little as three cents; full service for four could be bought for $1.99. In the years before World War II, depression glass was nationally distributed as advertising premiums.

Collectors today enjoy depression glass for a variety of reasons. It is available and easy to collect. Complete table services may be found in the same pattern and color. With a minimum of care, depression glass may be used without fear of permanent damage; pieces are replaceable.

Here is a list of depression glass patterns and manufacturers. These patterns are available in full or nearly full service sets. Prices vary and are unavailable. To date, they remain relatively low. Of greater value are the Royal Lace, Cherry Blossom, Manhattan Glass, and American Sweetheart patterns.

COLLECTIBLE GLASSWARE: DEPRESSION GLASS

FEDERAL GLASS CO.

PATTERN	DESCRIPTION	COLORS
Diana	Tableware with fine swirled lines, leading out from the center; rims slightly larger, curved lines	Pink, amber, and crystal
Georgian	Heavy glass in a lovebird motif	Green
Madrid	Mold-etched pattern	Pink, green, blue, amber, and crystal
Normandie	Alternating lattice and floral designs, center design a bouquet of flowers	Pink, amber iridescent orange, green, and crystal
Patrician	Eight-spoked design, surrounded by ten-point star shape	Pink, green, and amber
Sharon	Off-center motif of curved cabbage roses	Pink, green, and amber
Sylvan	Scenic pattern of parrots on bamboo branches	Green and amber

HAZEL ATLAS CO.

PATTERN	DESCRIPTION	COLORS
Florentine	Round plates with poppy border	Pink, green, yellow, and crystal
Moderntone	Simple, modern glassware designs	Burgundy and cobalt blue
Old Florentine	Six-sided plate with scalloping between the straight edges	Pink, green, yellow, and crystal
Royal Lace	Elaborate, modern design	Pink, green, crystal, cobalt blue, and burgundy

INDIANA GLASS CO.

PATTERN	DESCRIPTION	COLORS
Lorain	Square plates with cutoff scalloped edges, center motif of scrolls and garlands	Green, yellow, and crystal
Pineapple and Floral	Irregular scalloped edges around a center design of flowers and pineapples	Pink, green, teal, amber, and crystal

HOCKING GLASS CO.

PATTERN	DESCRIPTION	COLORS
Block Optic	Wide, concentric circles, set apart by blocks	Pink, yellow, and green
Cameo	Little dancing girls in plate borders, surrounded by bows and festoons	Pink, yellow, and green
Colonial	Traditional knife and fork pattern	Pink, green, crystal, and opaque cream
Lace Edge	Pressed pattern with open border design	Pink and crystal
Mayfair	Circles of roses	Pink, green, blue, topaz, and crystal
Princess	Snowflake design with spokes, lines, flowers, and leaves forming the border	Pink, green, topaz, and crystal
Queen Mary	Pressed, vertical, ribbed pattern	Pink and crystal
Sandwich	An elaborate arrangement of flowers, foliage and scrolls	Pink
Waterford	Radial lines, interrupted by circles of small blocks	Pink

JEANETTE GLASS CO.

PATTERN	DESCRIPTION	COLORS
Adam	Center design of flowers and plumes, rim decorated with flowers and foliage	Pink, green, and crystal

JEANETTE GLASS CO.

PATTERN	DESCRIPTION	COLORS
Cherry Blossom	Round plates with scalloped rims, center design of cherries and leaves, 12 panels of cherry blossoms	Pink, green, crystal, and opaque blue
Doric	Classic glass pattern. Star and loop design	Pink, green, crystal, opaque blue, and white
Doric and Pansy	Doric design with pansies filling the open spaces	Pink, crystal, and ultramarine
Floral	Passionflowers in the center, surrounded by alternating large leaves and flowers	Pink, crystal, and emerald green
Homespun	Waffle design with ribbed border	Pink, crystal, and blue
Windsor	Diamond-shaped facets to imitate cut crystal	Green, pink, and crystal

MACBETH EVANS GLASS CO.

PATTERN	DESCRIPTION	COLORS
American Sweetheart	Center arrangement of festoons, ribbons and scrolls	Pink and translucent white
Dogwood	Floral pattern with large blossoms and foliage	Pink, green, and crystal
Petalware	Center design of concentric circles, with scalloped edges	Pink, crystal, and "monax"
S Pattern	Leaves and stippling design scrolled edge	Yellow-gold, red, pink, crystal, and "monax"
Thistle	Thistles and foliage form center and border design	Pink, crystal, and emerald green

Dolls

Although doll prices have risen steadily in recent years, they may still often be found, for a pittance, at garage sales and flea markets. This is especially true of those dolls made in the twenties, thirties, and forties, whose values have yet to reach their peaks. Yet because the more valuable dolls are often unattainable except at high prices, observers of the collecting scene are setting their sights on a related item: teddy bears. It is expected that their prices will rise steadily in the next few years.

The following are some of the more notable dolls:

NAME	DATE	DESCRIPTION	CURRENT PRICE
Tête Jumeau	1842–99	Blue-eyed, bisque head	up to $800
Bisque head	1910	Bisque head, wooden body	up to $265
Minerva	1894	Tin head, kid body, bisque hands	up to $125
Frozen Charlotte	1850	Pillarlike doll with immobile limbs	up to $125
Schoenhut	1911	Wooden, with steel spring	up to $375
Palmer Cox's Brownie	late 1800s	Elflike rag doll (Indian, Irishman, policeman and dude)	up to $50
Campbell kids	1910	Molded heads and hands, cloth body	up to $250
Porcupine family	1910	Plush toys with name tags and labels of Steiff Toy Co.	up to $230
Kewpie dolls	1913	Bisque dolls with name "Kewpie" printed on heart	up to $125
Bye-Lo baby	1922	Bisque head, cloth body	up to $275
Teddy bear	1902	Movable legs and arms, humpbacked	up to $125

Condition is especially important in evaluating dolls. Since these are often the product of child mishandling, mint condition dolls are a true find and command high premiums. Doll clothing is also a fast-growing category of collectibles. Intricate, handmade fashions fetch higher prices and interest than commercially made garments.

Look carefully for handwork on dolls represented as early examples. Many reproductions flood the market and are sold at flea markets as the first edition. Even a tyro can spot the difference on close examination. The newer products do not have the stiching, screening, and painting that only hand detailing can produce.

Knives—The Cutting Collectible

Knives are for sporting, fishing, camping, sailing, and decoration. Though the first special hunting knife was made in the sixteenth century, it was not until after World War I that a trend appeared in specialized equipment. Since that day, knife crafting has become finer, as more and more qualified professionals have entered the market.

Below is a list of some old and some new respected (and collectible) names in knife making. Keep in mind that in this category the big growth is still to come in knives presently being manufactured. The best guides are design and feel. Unusual handles made of limited-supply material offer investment potential. Look also to the aesthetics rather than service. Modern technology can produce a perfect knife (if cutting is the measure of perfection) rather inexpensively. The value of a knife as a collectible relates to the amount of fascination it arouses.

KNIVES

COMPANY	DESCRIPTION	ESTIMATED CURRENT VALUE
Chappel, Rod	Knives, bowies, and fancy daggers	$90– $380
Dennehy, Dan	Fighting knives	$42– $180
D'Holder	Exotic materials used— amber, ivory, and inlaid turquoise	$44– $152
Frank, Henry	Ivory or horn covers and intricate engraving	$170– $470
Moran, William, Jr.	Classic knives, made with grips in precious metals and inlaid with gold or silver thread	$120/inch of blade
Smith, John T.	Highly polished, "clean" work, with fine bevel lines	$52– $168
Wiggins, Horace	Uses pieces of abalone, with seashells and fortified cactus for handles	$32– $72

Magazines

Pity the poor magazine collector. His dream is to pay for his child's college education with the massive collection of *Reader's Digest*s he keeps neatly tied and bundled in his basement. Unfortunately, few magazines will ever yield profits greater than the 2¢-per-pound paid during paper drives. Magazines are simply printed in numbers too great to hold any potential appreciation.

Yet, magazines with special stories can sometimes rapidly

increase in price. For example, issues of *Playboy* with Dan Greenburg stories often bring a good premium. First issues (volume 1, number 1) of magazines on almost any subject are of some interest. And if trends continue, the new wave of science fiction magazines should be carefully wrapped in cellophane for possible increase in value.

Whereas twenty-year-old copies of *Ladies' Home Journal* seldom bring a flea market dealer more than 25¢, the same vintage science fiction publications easily command $3 and more. Today's interest in space may be just a passing fancy, but if you feel compelled to save any back-date publications, the category of science fiction holds the most promise.

Matchbook Covers

A fortune tomorrow from no cost today is every collector's dream. Ever since the book match began replacing the boxed safety match, inventive businessmen saw an opportunity for low-cost advertising. "Imagine," says the advertising matchbook salesman, "getting a prospect to look at your sales message twenty times for less than a penny."

Not far behind the advertising matchbook salesman came the advertising matchbook collector. Each year over a hundred million matchbooks are produced, many with interesting and unique advertising.

The key to collecting is to find matchbooks from interesting places. Eliminate those that have no design beauty or are in huge supply (e.g., Sheraton Hotels and "Finish High School at Home"). Instead, collect the ones that are limited, rare, or reflect your exotic travels. Collectors seek matchbooks from the White House, foreign countries, and especially formerly famous restaurants no longer existing.

Collecting matches is simple, since they are freely available. Tell friends about your hobby and they are likely to offer you valuable additions.

To save these collectibles, carefully remove the staple,

discard the matches, and flatten the book cover. You can then mount them in an album or loose-leaf binder.

Recently, so-called topical collections have begun to bring high prices. Covers that show flowers, birds, and animals are particularly popular. Trading offers a way to expand one's collection significantly and inexpensively.

Medals

Medals. Small, flat, usually circular pieces of bronze, silver or gold, made in limited quantities. Of ancient origin, they are decorated with designs and embossed, on both sides, in high or low relief.

Medals are time recorders, issued to commemorate events or to honor individuals. One medal, commemorating the founding of Constantinople in A.D. 32, is in a Paris collection. Today, Centennial limited editions continue to gain popularity. Since 1966, corresponding with the issuance of the John F. Kennedy commemoratives, medals have proved by their sales records to be the most satisfying and attractive limited editions to collect.

Several factors combine to explain this growing appeal. As the culminated effort of artists and craftsmen, medals are pampered in their making. As permanent works of art, they are handled and kept with care. Truly, many medals are limited editions, either by preannouncement or by the fact that few are struck before the die is destroyed.

The striking appearance and limited supply of medallic art feeds a high demand. Medals may often sell for a greater price than their original value. In sum, a medal is frequently a collectible for both profit and pleasure.

The following medals were issued only recently and may take several years to appreciate in value.

MEDALS

COMPANY	DESCRIPTION	CIRCULATION	ORIGINAL COST	CURRENT VALUE (WHEN AVAILABLE)
Franklin Mint Medals	Holiday and commemorative medals issued in sterling silver and prooflike editions	55 different series 1970–72 250–120,382	$5–$570	$30–$650
Franklin Mint Ingots (metal bars)	Commemorative, holiday, and historic ingots	8 different series 1970–72 906–47,912	$11–$515/ set of 50	$12–$550/ set of 50
Franklin Mint International Series	Art medals, commemorating European heads of state	3 different series 1972 952–1,741	$171/set–$210/set	$175/set–$215/set
Indian Tribal Series	Silver- and proof-finish medals, made by Franklin Mint	1 series 1971, 1972 4,500	$15–$16	$16–$17.50
The International Mint	Commemorative medals in sterling, fine silver, and prooflike editions	4 different series 1970–72 400–3,200	$9.75–$12.00	$9.75–$12.00

International Numismatic Agency	High relief medals issued in bronze or sterling silver	12 different series 1969–73 500–15,000	$25– $175/set	$25–$175/set
Judaic Heritage Society	Historical documentation on bronze or sterling medals	2 different series 1969–73 630–1,858	$9.50– (sterling price not available)	$9.50–$16.00 (sterling price not available)
The Lincoln Mint	Commemorative medals covering a wide subject range	9 different series 1970–74 1,000–7,500	$8.50– $35.00	$9.50–$32.00
Medallic Art Co.	High relief medals, struck in various materials	1 series 1972 15,000	$14.75	$14.75
Presidential Art Medals, Inc.	High relief, commemorative medals, struck in platinum, silver, or bronze	8 different series 1972 2,500–10,000	$11– $35	$11–$45

Miniatures

Originally used only as children's playthings, miniatures are fast becoming adult collectibles. Today just about anything available in a regular home is also made for the miniature house, but the most valuable miniature items are those made before the craze of the 70s began.

The following is a list of some miniatures:

ITEM	DATE	DESCRIPTION	CURRENT PRICE
Big Little Books (Whitman Publishing)	1920s–30s	Subjects included comic strip, movie, and real-life heros	$4.50 to $20.00 (and expected to rise)
Brass bed (French manufacturer)	1890s	Bamboo motif in bed frame (upholstered mattress)	up to $175
W. Britains, Ltd.	1915–39	Mounted Scots Greys Band	up to $200
Cast iron	1870s	Miniature cradles, rockers	up to $85 each
Little Blue Books	1920–40	Over 2,000 titles, including Shakespeare, 19th-century classics, and original books	$2.50 each (original price 10¢)
Lynnfield	1930s	Art Deco–style maple wood furniture	up to $50 for single item
Salesmen's samples	1800s	Slightly larger furniture miniatures (used as samples by salesmen)	up to $700
Staffordshire "Hackford"	1800s	Set of blue and white patterned dinnerware	$40 to $60 per item
Tynietoy	1924–50	Miniature wooden furniture	up to $950 for box; up to $100 for single item

No one knows exactly what accounts for the miniature frenzy. Yet some say today's small houses and apartments mean less space to collect in, and some collectors just want anything if it's small. They currently save miniature calculators and even tiny televisions. It's best to save miniatures that have dual collectibility (e.g., miniature furniture that is for mini collectors but appeals to dollhouse collectors as well).

Mugs and Steins

Mugs and steins were traditionally part of a table setting. Though none were originally intended to be designed as restricted issues, some have acquired the same attribute of rarity that characterizes the limited edition.

Mugs and steins appear to have originated around the fourteenth century. These deep, straight-handled cups may be made of wood, glass, metal, or ceramics, and have long been associated with the drinking of beer and ale.

Usually created for presentation, mugs and steins from Germany are often elegant works of art, hand-carved in ivory or precious metal. Painted, ceramic mugs are most often mass-produced, as they were intended for the beer halls of Europe and America.

It was not until 1967 that the Royal Copenhagen Porcelain Company publicized and distributed the first limited edition of stoneware mugs, in pint and half-pint sizes. The edition was limited with respect to time only, and was characterized by the use of the year in the design composition.

Though not as popular as limited-edition plates, mugs and steins are still valuable collectibles. They currently are underpriced and should enjoy a rapid rise in the near future.

MUGS AND STEINS

COMPANY	DESCRIPTION	CIRCULATION	ORIGINAL COST	CURRENT VALUE
Berlin Design	Porcelain-coated beer steins, picturing German castles Released annually	Series of 3 1971–73 700	$40	$38
Noritake	Fine porcelain, Mother's Day and Father's Day mugs Released annually	Series of 2 1973 Not available	$15–$20	$14–$18
Porsgrund	Christmas and Father's Day mugs	Series of 6 1970–73	$11–$20	$11–$22
Royal Copenhagen	Various-sized porcelain mugs, limited only by the quantity sold in one year	Series of 7 1967–73 Not available	$25–$27	$25–$38
Royal Doulton	Charles Dickens commemorative ceramic Christmas tankards and loving cups	Series of 2 1970–73 500–15,000	$35–$285	$40–$275
Schmid & Hummel	Painted porcelain child's cup	Series of 1 1973 Not available	$10	$8
Schuler	Pewter Christmas tankard, hand-painted in oils	Series of 1 1973 500	$55	$53
Wedgwood	Jasperware and porcelain commemorative and Christmas mugs	Series of 8 1966–72 200–4,000	$20–$30	Not available

Pens

The early fountain pen is still one of the most underpriced collectibles. The future holds great promise for this art object. Maurice Winston sells and repairs old pens in a New York shop (The Authorized Repair Service, Inc.). He says it best: "An antique pen had perfect balance. They were beautiful to hold and look at, and they put character and beauty into writing."

Louis E. Waterman is generally credited with designing the first workable fountain pen. An eyedropper was used to fill the interior barrel of the pen. His monopoly in the 1800s was ended in the early 1900s when George Parker began to compete in this new market. The early Parker pens were quite stylish, and although they are in relatively short supply can frequently be found at country auctions and flea markets.

The pen often has intrinsic meaning beyond its function as a writing instrument. For example, pens used by elected officials to sign a bill into law are often mounted on plaques and given as mementos to important friends of the legislation.

The way to make money in pen collectibles is to buy non-working instruments, which are often sold inexpensively. These can be do-it-yourself repaired with a minimum of study; for intricate work, use any of the various city "pen hospitals." One excellent source that will fix pens by mail is M. C. Flynn, Inc., 43 East 59th Street, New York, N.Y. 10022.

The following is a small selection of collectible fountain pens and their current prices:

Waterman Sterling Barrel	$20
Waterman 14K gold	$35
Waterman (with original eyedropper)	$50

Plates

Limited-edition, commemorative, and celebration plates have been issued in porcelain, pottery, or crystal. Some have even been struck in gold or silver. Others, from Germany, are intricately carved in wood.

The first true limited-edition Christmas plate was issued in 1895 by the Bing and Grondhal Company of Denmark. Since that time, this company has released well over one hundred thousand annually, producing plates only through July. Traditionally all master molds are destroyed in a Christmas Eve ceremony. The Bing and Grondhal Christmas plates are the largest well-known restricted editions in the world. The illustrated, under-glazed, blue and white porcelain plates are easily recognizable.

In 1908 the Royal Copenhagen Porcelain Company joined in the production of annual Christmas plates. These plates were characterized by their illustrated, underglazed blue, and marked on the back with a trade symbol of three wavy lines.

Today, sales records indicate an increasing trend toward collecting limited-edition plates. Most responsible for this is Lalique, the French jeweler and glass producer. In 1965 Lalique released the first annual plate, a small limited edition in the Lalique style of elevated, iced design on a clear crystal background. Within months the original price of $25 had risen by hundreds of dollars. Similar price increases are not uncommon in this area, as you will see in the chart that follows.

COMPANY	DESCRIPTION	CIRCULATION	ORIGINAL COST	CURRENT VALUE (WHERE AVAILABLE)
Count Agazzi of Venice, Inc.	Reversed painting on signed, Venetian glass plate	Series of 8 1968–73 600–2,000	$8–$35	$12.50–$45.00
Arlington Mint	Silver and gold collector's plate, picturing "Hands in Prayer"	1972 Not available	$125	$120
Belleek	Delicate porcelain Christmas plates	Series of 3 1970–72 5,000–7,500	$25–$35	$35–$122
Paul Briant & Sons	24K-gold-plated, photo-engraved plates, marked on the back by traditional elephant and thumbprint	Series of 2 1971, 1972 350–700	$85–$150	$85–$145
Cartier	Plates in fine porcelain and sterling silver	Series of 2 1972, 1973 500 and 12,500	$50–$250	$50–$245
Crown Staffordshire	Fine English ceramic plates	Series of 2 1972, 1973 10,000	$25.00–$27.50	$25–$26
Dorothy Doughty dessert plates Royal Worcester	Intricate bas-relief and hand-painted plates	First series 1972 2,000	$125	$389

PLATES (Continued)

COMPANY	DESCRIPTION	CIRCULATION	ORIGINAL COST	CURRENT VALUE (WHEN AVAILABLE)
Fenton Art Glass Co.	Carnival blue milk or white milk glass commemorative plates	Series of 3 1970–73 Not available	$10.00– $12.50	$10–$17
Franklin Mint Plates	Uniform, 8-inch-diameter sterling silver plate with etched design	Series of 7 1970–72 10,304–24,792	$100– $150	$125–$490
Haviland & Co.	Fine porcelain china services, many generations old. Also, commemorative plates	Series of 4 1973–76 2,500–30,000	$30– $110	$30–$165
Hutschenreuther	Christmas plate by Juan Ferrandiz	Series of 2 1972, 1973 3,000 and 5,000	$30	$25
Georg Jensen	Ceramic Christmas and commemorative plates, marked by distinctive border and Jensen trademark (with one exception)	Series of 3 1972, 1973 Not available	$15– $50	$15–$45
Arthur King	4-inch distinctively hammered plates of precious metals	Series of 2 1972, 1973 750	$325– $400	$325–$390

H. H. Lihs	7½-inch cobalt porcelain plates, etched in 24K gold	Series of 5 1972, 1973 1,000–6,000	$25– $55	$30–$45
Louis Lourioux	9½-inch tinted porcelain plate bordered in gold Discontinued	First series 1971 7,500	Not available	$12
Kay Malleck	Christmas plates designed by American Indian artists	Series of 5 1971–73 500–2,000	$15– $17	$14
Orrefors	Commemorative and Mother's Day plates of modern design with etched lines filled with gold	Series of 2 1970–73 Not available	$45– $50	$45–$51
Porcelain de Paris	Hand-enameled plates in rich colors picturing the Chinese apostles of Lao-tse	Series of 2 1973 300	$175/set of 4	$172/set of 4
Ram	Commemorative and holiday plates	Series of 2 1972 500–1,000	$7.95– $30.00	$7.95–$28.00
Roskilde	Christmas plates, picturing Danish churches	Series of 3 1968–71 Not available	$8– $10	$15–$22

PLATES (Continued)

COMPANY	DESCRIPTION	CIRCULATION	ORIGINAL COST	CURRENT VALUE (WHEN AVAILABLE)
Royal Worcester	10½-inch pewter plate with deep bas-relief center, commemorating U.S. Bicentennial	Series of 2 1972, 1973 Not available	$45	$44
Selandia	8¼-inch pewter Christmas plates designed by artist John Gulbrandsrod	Series of 3 1972, 1973 250–4,750	$35– $100	$35–$99
Franz Stanek	Copperwheel engraved commemorative plates	Series of 3 1969, 1972 60–150	$600– $1,000	$600–$970
Towle	10½-inch sterling silver Christmas plates	Series of 2 1972, 1973 2,500	$7.95– $250.00	$7.95–$230.00
George Washington Mint	Commemorative plates on precious metals	Series of 6 1972, 1973 100–9,800	$125– $2,000	$125–$1,980
Josiah Wedgwood	Jasperware commemorative Christmas and Mother's Day plates	Series of 7 1968–73 Not available	$7.95– $30.00	$8–$98

Playing Cards

The legend and history of playing cards are filled with romance and intrigue. Very early decks were simply miniature works of art that were the exclusive property of the very wealthy. Their popularity grew as modern printing technology brought the price down within the reach of most households.

The first producer of American playing cards was Jaz Ford of Milton, Massachusetts. His cards were thought to be so inferior to the popular British cards that he imprinted them "Made in London" to mislead the buyer. Cards from England and United States dating back to the late 1800s are frequently offered today at reasonable prices.

Early playing cards make a good investment, as they combine the interests of antique collectors and art students, as well as those interested in games and gambling. Early cards tend to be more pictorial and colorful than those currently available. It is important that the buyer carefully check a deck before purchase. The absence of a single card will render the deck worthless to a serious collector. Also, the original box (slipcase) is an important determinant of value. Early decks of children's cards have appreciated only slightly in the last decade and should be due for increases as demand outstrips the limited supply. Collectors should try especially to acquire children's cards that feature famous characters such as Mickey Mouse.

In terms of future investing, one should "tuck away" advertising playing cards that are widely distributed. Most airlines will provide free cards to travelers, and the cards from smaller regional carriers hold good potential (at no initial cost).

Records—The Contemporary Collectible

The record business is a multibillion-dollar industry, surpassing all other entertainment media. Its function is to develop, mass-produce, and market a product that is a work of art.

Rock music has become the dominant popular music form of the century. In its third decade, rock and roll has been produced by many artists on dozens of major and independent levels. Since the 1950s, records have been collected, catalogued, and studied. Sales indicators show several areas of interest. They are:

1955—the "doo wop" vocal group sound
1964—surfing music
1966—punk rock
1967—British progressive rock
1973—recent British rock

This diversification proves that record collecting is no longer merely a function of nostalgia. A record collection may be built around personal tastes or as a means of tracing roots in rock history. More and more, emphasis is being focused on record popularity, and records that are only two years old may be valuable collectibles.

The condition of a record is important in determining its value. A rare record, in near-mint condition, with its jacket, will demand the highest selling price. Anyone who thinks that collectibles have to be very old in order to gain in value need only look at the list that follows.

COLLECTIBLE RECORDS: THE MONEY RECORDS

Original 45s, in near-mint condition, and valued at more than $25, qualify as "money records." Below is a small sampling of what to look for:

ARTIST	TITLE	LABEL & NUMBER	ESTIMATED VALUE
Andrews, Lee & The Hearts	"Bells of St. Mary's"	Rainbow 259	$30
Andrews, Lee & The Hearts	"Long, Lonely Nights"	Mainline 102	$20

ARTIST	TITLE	LABEL & NUMBER	ESTIMATED VALUE
Andrews, Lee & The Hearts	"Maybe You'll Be There"	Rainbow 252	$55
Andrews, Lee & The Hearts	"White Cliffs of Dover"	Rainbow 250	$90
Barry, Jan	"Tomorrow's Teardrops"	Ripple 6101	$20
Beach Boys	"Surfin' "	"X" 301	$60
Beach Boys	"Surfin' "	Candix 301	$30
Beach Boys	"Surfin' "	Candix 331	$25
Beatles (released as Tony Sheridan & The Beat Brothers)	"My Bonnie"	Decca 31382	$400
Beatles	"Please, Please Me" (first U.S. release)	VeeJay 498	$125
Beatles	"Please, Please Me" (multicolor band) around the label)	VeeJay 498	$115
Beatles	"Please, Please Me" (Beatles misspelled "Beattles")	VeeJay 498	$90
Beatles	"She Loves You" (thick lettering, doesn't have "don't drop out")	Swan 4152	$90
Beatles	"She Loves You" (second printing, has "don't drop out" printed in thin letters)	Swan 4152	$90
Beatles	"Sie Liebt Dich" ("She Loves You")	Swan 5182	$30
Big Bopper	"Chantilly Lace"	D 1008	$25
Bob & Sheri (featuring Brian Wilson)	"The Surfer Moon"	Safari 101	$200
Capris	"There's a Moon Out Tonight"	Planet 1010	$45
Cochran Brothers	"Guilty Conscience"	Ekko 1002	$55
Cochran Brothers	"Two Blue Singing Stars"	Ekko 1003	$60

ARTIST	TITLE	LABEL & NUMBER	ESTIMATED VALUE
Cochran Brothers	"Tired and Sleepy"	Ekko 3001	$70
Dixon, Bill & The Topics	"I Am All Alone"	Topix 6003	$30
Domino, Fats	"Don't Lie to Me"	Imperial 5123	$32
Domino, Fats	"Every Night About This Time"	Imperial 5099	$35
Domino, Fats	"Right From Wrong"	Imperial 5138	$30
Domino, Fats	"Rockin' Chair"	Imperial 5145	$28
Domino, Fats	"Tired of Crying"	Imperial 5114	$32
Domino, Fats	"You Know I'll Miss You"	Imperial 5167	$25
Dominoes	"Sixty-Minute Man"	Federal 12022	$50
Dylan, Bob	"Blowin' in the Wind"	Columbia 42856	$40
Everett, Vince	"Baby, Let's Play House"	ABC Paramount 10472	$35
Everett, Vince	"I Ain't Gonna Be Your Low Down Dog No More"	ABC Paramount	$30
Five Satins	"I Remember (In The Still of the Night)"	Standard 200	$30
Five Sharps	"Stormy Weather"		$5,000
Flamingos	"I Really Don't Want to Know"		$200
Four Lovers (Four Seasons)	"My Life for Your Love"	Epic 9255	$50
Haley, Bill	"Green Tree Boogie"	Holiday 108	$35
Haley, Bill	"I'm Crying"	Holiday 110	$30
Haley, Bill	"Jukebox Cannonball"	Holiday 113	$28
Haley, Bill	"Rocket 88"	Holiday 105	$40
Hill, Joel	"Little Lover"	Trans-American 519	$25
Honeys	"Surfin' Down the Swanee River"	Capitol 4952	$25
Jan & Arnie	"Baby Talk"	Dore 522	$50
Joey & The Teenagers	"What's on Your Mind?"	Columbia 42054	$30
Johnnie & Joe	"Over the Mountain and Across the Sea"	J & S 1654	$30
King, Carole	"Oh, Neil"	Alpine 57	$25
Little Richard	"Every Hour"	RCA 4392	$50
Little Richard	"Get Rich Quick"	RCA 4582	$40

ARTIST	TITLE	LABEL & NUMBER	ESTIMATED VALUE
Little Richard	"Please Have Mercy on Me"	RCA 5025	$30
Little Richard	"Why Did You Leave Me?"	RCA 4722	$40
Love, Darlene	"He's a Quiet Guy"	Phillies 123	$25
Luman, Bob	"Red Hot"	Imperial 8313	$30
O'Ryan, Jack & Al Tercek	"Political Circus" (Part One)	Nocturne P-8	$35
Perkins, Carl	"Gone, Gone, Gone"	Sun 224	$30
Perkins, Carl	"Movie Magg"		$75
Presley, Elvis	"Good Rockin' Tonight"	Sun 210	$270
Presley, Elvis	"I'm Left, You're Right, She's Gone"	Sun 217	$230
Presley, Elvis	"Milkcow Blues Boogie"	Sun 215	$310
Presley, Elvis	"Mystery Train"	Sun 223	$180
Roulettes	"Hasten Jason"	Sceptor 1204	$25
Scott, Jack	"Baby, She's Gone"	ABC Paramount 9819	$25
Scott, Jack	"Two-Timin' Woman"	ABC Paramount	$25
Sha-Weez	"No One to Love Me"		$200
Sheridan, Tony & The Beat Brothers (Beatles)	"My Bonnie"	Decca 31382	$500
Swallows	"Since You've Been Away"		$150
The Vocaleers	"Shim Sham Shimmy"		$2,500

Records in good condition, showing some signs of wear and some foreign noises, will generally be valued at half the near-mint price. The above is a sampling of the rarer records. The average value of most other collectible records is between $2 and $7.

You may be among those fortunate enough to find rare recording cylinders, the original "records," or to even possess an album or 78 that is now a rarity. Below are just a few of the records worth more than their original list prices.

TITLE	DATE	DESCRIPTION	CURRENT PRICE
Bettini wax cylinders	1899	One of the first "records"; many of these also have historical value.	up to $300 each (original cost $6)
Damn Yankees (with Gwen Verdon)	1955	Original cover showed Gwen in baseball shirt and hat	$20
Beatles *Yesterday and Today*	1965	First cover had pictures of broken dolls alongside Beatles; very few albums with this cover were released.	$100–$150
Elvis Presley Christmas album	1957	Contains color photos of Elvis inside.	$60
Baby Mack "You've Got to Get Home on Time" (OKEH 8313-B) (78 rpm)	1926	Valuable because it is one of first recordings to feature Louis Armstrong.	up to $150

Spoons and Forks

Sterling silver flatware passed from family to family before it was considered a collector's item. It was not until the late nineteenth century that the "memory" or "souvenir" spoon was introduced to celebrate special events. Though these spoons were signed and dated, they were never intended as limited editions. Today they join with specifically designed, restricted issues to offer a selection of decorative collectibles.

SPOONS

COMPANY	DESCRIPTION	CIRCULATION	ORIGINAL COST	CURRENT VALUE
Franklin Mint spoons	Zodiac and Twelve Days of Christmas spoons	Two different series 1972 5,386 Not available	$135/set $145/set	$133/set $144/set
Gorham Christmas spoons	Sterling silver spoons of distinctive design, with different handle designs each year.	Only one series 1972 Not available	$10	$8
Kirk Christmas spoons	4⅛-inch Christmas spoons in sterling silver (or 14K gold)	First series 1972 81 and 6,000	$12.50 (or $125)	$12.50 (or $122)
A. Michelsen	6-inch sterling silver Christmas and commemorative spoons, decorated with inlaid enamel	Three different series 1910–72 Not available	Not available	$27– $70

Sporting Art—Paintings, Prints, and Etchings

There has always been a connection between art and sport. In early days, art was a way to capture and preserve the spirit of the hunt, the prey, and, finally, the moment of conquest. In England, art recorded sport as a social pastime for country squires. Years later, in America, where sport was often a means of survival, art would record the frontiersman and his food.

True art has different value for each individual. But sporting art offers a limitless range of subjects, styles, and prices to appeal to almost any collector. The quality of reproduction is a key element. For example, a Currier and Ives print can be had for under $5. A collector will only want one in which the printing was done by Currier and Ives. As with all art, watch out for reproductions being passed off as originals. Buy only from a recognized dealer who offers a certificate or other guarantee.

SPORTING ART

ARTIST	MEDIUM	DESCRIPTION	ESTIMATED CURRENT VALUE
Adamson, Harry C.	Prints	Limited editions, issued from 1971–74, of wild game fowl	$50–$360
Audubon, John James	Paintings	Skillful depictions of wildlife in natural settings, especially *Birds of America* Extremely rare	$45,000 (average value)
Bierly, Edward J.	Prints	Limited editions, issued from 1969–74, depicting African wildlife	$45–$54
Bishop, Richard	Paintings (also watercolors, oils, and pen and ink)	Best known are the waterfowl paintings	$360–$1,350
Bull, Charles L.	Paintings	Marked by the extreme detail given to animal anatomy	$1,800–$9,000
Clark, Roland	Etchings (also dry paints, watercolors and oils)	Limited-edition etchings depicting waterfowl with lifelike authenticity	$135–$1,080
Coheleach, Guy	Paintings	Most often picture African wildlife	$23,000 maximum
Currier and Ives	Prints	Sporting prints in a portfolio	$110–$5,400
Fernely, John	Paintings	Characterized by the activity of the scene; reproduce the foxhunt and its spirit	$1,800–$36,000
Frost, Arthur	Prints	Marked by a delicate use of color to portray hunting and fishing scenes	$225–$1,350
Hagerbaumer, David	Paintings	Watercolors used to depict wildfowl and upland game fowl	$1,000–$4,050

SPORTING ART (Continued)

ARTIST	MEDIUM	DESCRIPTION	ESTIMATED CURRENT VALUE
Homer, Winslow	Paintings	Authentic documentation of the Adirondack and Canadian woodlands, using strong colors and tone	$5,400–$405,000
King, Edward	Prints	Limited editions, prints depicting hunting and racing	$90–$900
Knap, J. D.	Paintings	Best recognized by watercolor depictions of waterfowl	$180–$1,350
Maas, David	Prints	Limited-edition prints of waterfowl and upland game birds	$45–$1,000
Megargee, Edward	Paintings	Dogs and upland shooting painted in oil colors	$720–$2,250
Peterson, Roger Tory	Paintings	Birds, in detail, and in their environment; contemporary	$2,250–$9,000
Pleissner, Ogden M.	Prints (also paintings)	Limited-edition prints portraying all aspects of the sporting world	$135–$900
Reece, Maynard	Paintings	Fish and game, painted in their natural habitat	$5,400–$10,800
Ripley, Lassell A.	Prints (also paintings)	Prints portray the energy of the hunt	$45–$1,080
Rungius, Carl	Paintings	Portrayals of North American wildlife	$5,400–$45,000
Schaldach, William J.	Paintings	Oil paintings of big African game	to $22,500
Stubbs, George	Paintings	Realistic studies of animal life	$10,800–$180,000
Voss, Franklin B.	Prints	Limited-edition prints of fox-hunting	$110–$675

Sporting Collectibles—Firearms

Firearm collections have grown rapidly in appeal and value in the past twenty years. Manufactured in a variety of grades and qualities, there are firearms to satisfy just about any kind of collector.

Below is a small sample list of firearms and their manufacturers.

COMPANY	DESCRIPTION	ESTIMATED CURRENT VALUE
Baker	Batavia shotgun	$200–$345
Beretta	Golden snipe shotgun	$440
Browning	.22 caliber, automatic rifle; three grades	$80–$340
Hunter Arms	Double-barreled shotgun	$200–$240
Iver Johnson	Double-barreled shotgun	$150–$390
Marlin	Lever-, pump-, and bolt-action rifles	$18–$480
Mauser	Bolt-action rifles	$235–$440
Mossberg	Bold action shotgun	$25–$45
Parker	Single- and double-barreled shotguns	$240–$1,700
Remington	Slide- and bolt-action rifles	$70–$170
Savage	Lever-action rifles	$90–$280
L.C. Smith	Field-grade double-barreled shotgun	$170–$390
Weatherby	Bolt-action rifles	$170–$390
Winchester	Pump shotgun; three models	$140–$390
Winchester	Slide-, lever-, auto-, and bolt-action rifles	$80–$730

Sporting Collectibles—Rods and Reels

Rods and reels are indispensable to the fisherman, but they're just as valuable—and profitable—to the interested collector.

The most significant factor in determining their value is

condition. By the nature of their use, rods and reels have a heavy wear factor. Some basic knowledge of fishing equipment is required, as many rods and reels look similar. Company names often do not appear on the rods.

Here is a list of representative facts and figures for rods and reels.

RODS

COMPANY	SIZE AND DESCRIPTION	ESTIMATED CURRENT VALUE
Dickerson, Lyle	$7\frac{1}{2}$- to 10-foot rods at $3\frac{1}{2}$ to $6\frac{1}{4}$ ounces Marked by fast-action performance	$180–$315
Edwards, Eustis	6- to $9\frac{1}{2}$-foot rods in two- and three-piece designs Dark-bamboo with yellow-tipped, purple wraps	$110–$270
Garrison, Everett	7- to 8-foot rods at 2 to 4 ounces Rods were built of split cane	$540–$720
Gillium, Harold Steele	$7\frac{1}{2}$- to $8\frac{1}{2}$-foot rods with fast tapers Black glue lines prominent	$315–$720
Granger, Goodwin	7- to $9\frac{1}{2}$-foot rods, marked by brown cane and a full-Wells handle	$68–$150
Halstead, George	Rare	$225–$360
Heddon, James & Sons	$7\frac{1}{2}$- to 9-foot rods	$110–$225
Jordon, Wes	Most rods made with a screw-locking reel seat	$90–$135

RODS (Continued)

COMPANY	SIZE AND DESCRIPTION	ESTIMATED CURRENT VALUE
Leonard, Hiram Lewis	7½- to 10-foot rods Better rods are rare	$210–$450

Payne, Edward	8- to 10-foot rods at
	   3¼ to 6 ounces
	Brown-tone sticks were
	   the Payne trademark
		$270–$495

Phillipson, Bill	7½- to 9-foot rods at 3¼ to 6 ounces	$68–$120

Powell, Edwin	7½- to 9½-foot rods at
	   3½ to 6 ounces
	Wrapped in brown
	   or antique gold
	Signed
		$135–$270

The South Bend Bait Co.	7- to 9-foot rods	$68–$135
Thomas, Fred	7½- to 15-foot rods Soft-action rods in straw or brown cane	$110–$290
Thomas & Thomas	6½- to 8½-foot rods	$162–$290
Winchester Rod Co., The R.L.	5½- to 8½-foot rods at 2¼ to 5½ ounces Two-piece design	$135–$200

REELS

COMPANY	SIZE AND DESCRIPTION	YEAR MADE	ESTIMATED CURRENT VALUE
Billinghurst, William	Nickel-plated, birdcage fly or trolling reel	1869	$150–$200
Coxe, J. A.	Aluminum casting reel	1940	$75–$100
Leonard, H. L.	Bronze or silver, 2½-by-1-inch fly reel	1877	$360–$450
Meek, J. F. & B. F.	Silver casting reel	1900	$60–$90
Milam, B. C.	Short-handled casting reel, made in brass	1865	$315–$405
Pfleuger	5-by-1-inch brass trolling reel	1915	$18
Sage, J. L.	Pure silver click fly reel	1848	$675
Snyder, George	1¾-by-1⅞-inch multiplying brass casting reel	1820	$360–$540
South Bend	Aluminum fly reel	1940	$22
Talbot, William	Silver casting reel	1920	$60–$80
Von Hofe, J.	Small-sized nickel and rubber, fly reel	1890	$90–$135
Yawman & Erbe	Automatic, aluminum fly reel	1889	$78–$110
Zwarg, Otto	Black rubber marlin reel	1905	$135–$180

Stained-Glass Windows

Stained glass appeared in churches as early as the sixth century. It was originally obtained by adding metals to glass during the manufacturing process. Although stained-glass windows are widely produced today, they do not have the artistry and aesthetics of early glass.

Stained glass has significant investment potential and is still available at prices affordable by many collectors. The would-be buyer need not be overly concerned about fakes, since a simple study will clearly indicate the difference in quality between majestic favrile glass and painted panes sold to unwary buyers.

Small windows are still sold for as little as $200 and on occasion can be purchased from wrecking companies. As recently as 1950 they could be purchased for the same price as clear glass. Stained glass tends to be highly fragile, so the collector must exercise the utmost care in storage.

Stamps—Federal Duck Stamps

The first Federal Duck Stamp was issued in 1934 and has been issued yearly since. All designs are from Federal Migratory Waterfowl Stamp Prints, and are done by well-known sporting artists.

FEDERAL DUCK STAMP PRINTS

YEAR ISSUED	ARTIST	TITLE	ESTIMATED CURRENT VALUE
1934	Darling, Ding	"Mallards"	$1,575
1937	Knap, J. D.	"Broadbills"	$1,440
1940	Jacques, F. L.	"Black Ducks"	$3,375 first and second editions
1943	Bohl	"Wood Ducks"	$675 first edition
1946	Hines	"Red Heads"	$1,260
1949	Preuss	"Golden Eyes"	$1,350

YEAR ISSUED	ARTIST	TITLE	ESTIMATED CURRENT VALUE
1952	Dick	"Harlequins"	$810
1955	Stearns, S.	"Blue Geese"	$675 first edition
1958	Kouba	"Canada Geese"	$675 first edition
1961	Morris	"Mallard Family"	$585
1964	Stearns, S.	"Nene Geese"	$630 first edition
1967	Kouba	"Old Squaws"	$540
1970	Bierly, E.	"Ross's Geese"	$630 ✗700 & below
1973	LeBlanc, L.	"Steller's Eider"	$630 first edition

Federal Duck Stamp prints have long been a collector's item. They are usually issued in limited numbers and editions. A complete set of prints sells for $55,000; a complete set of stamps for about $900. Consult your local post office or stamp dealer for further information.

Collectors often look for both stamp and print. Stamps may be best displayed in a frame, with the corresponding print. Here is a sample list:

FEDERAL DUCK STAMPS

YEAR ISSUED	DENOMINATION & DESCRIPTION	SUBJECT	ESTIMATED CURRENT VALUE, UNUSED
1934	$1.00 blue	Mallards	$50.00
1937	$1.00 light green	Broadbills	$25.00
1940	$1.00 sepia	Black ducks	$27.00
1943	$1.00 deep rose	Wood ducks	$19.00
1946	$1.00 red brown	Red-headed ducks	$11.00
1949	$2.00 bright green	Golden-eyed ducks	$14.00
1952	$2.00 deep ultramarine	Harlequin ducks	$14.00
1955	$2.00 dark blue	Geese	$13.50
1958	$2.00 black	Canadian geese	$13.50
1961	$3.00 blue, brown	Mallard family	$29.00
1964	$3.00 blue, black, brown	Nene geese	$50.00
1967	$3.00 multicolored	Old squaws	$45.00
1970	$3.00 multicolored	Geese	$20.00
1973	$5.00 multicolored	Eider	$ 8.50

Used Federal Duck Stamps are valued at one-third to one-half the unused price.

Stocks, Deeds, and Canceled Checks

Can the collector really spend five dollars today and have a collectible that yields hundreds in a few years? The answer is a qualified yes. With the rush to collecting, some discarded checks and stock certificates have been transformed from worthless paper into valuable Americana.

In the case of checks, the secret is to look for endorsements that are worthwhile as autographs. The great writers of our time created not only novels and letters but checks as well. Flea markets will often offer cartons of checks for a few dollars. A careful reading of them will unearth some potentially rare signatures. Although some famous people had others sign their letters, few failed to sign their own checks. Recently a collector told me of an ugly chest he purchased for $25. The dealer thought he had really unloaded something better junked. The collector actually did throw away the chest because what he was after were the checks and deeds stuffed in each of the drawers.

Deeds and other business certificates offer similar opportunity. Stock certificates of now-defunct companies have interest and value due to economic significance. The fine lithography associated with stock issues makes them beautiful as an art form. They are so inexpensive now (frequently as little as 25¢ each) that they are sure to appreciate in value.

CHECKS	CURRENT PRICE
P. T. Barnum	25.00
Samuel Clemens (Mark Twain)	100.00
Andrew Jackson	100.00
John F. Kennedy	1,000.00
Brigham Young	100.00

CHECKS	CURRENT PRICE
STOCKS & BONDS	
Horse-drawn car company stock	5.00
Most defunct companies	1.00
Railroad stock	2.00

Theater Programs

A collection of theater programs will cost you nothing to start and offer an exciting future. If you live in New York or visit there often, the collection is at your fingertips. Every Broadway show offers free programs listing the cast and other information about the particular shows.

The covers alone are sometimes collected and framed for their attractive art. Interestingly, most people leave their programs behind at the conclusion of the show. It is a simple task to pass through the theater and pick up hundreds of them. One collector using this technique amassed large numbers of programs from the few shows he had seen. Then it became a simple matter to trade with other collectors who did not hold the program of a particular production.

The future collectibility will combine both the famous and the short-lived. Most collectors will want a program from a hit such as *My Fair Lady*, but because it ran for years they are quite plentiful in collectors' circles. To obtain rare Broadway programs, obtain opening-night tickets. In this way, you may acquire one of the few printed souvenirs of a production that closes after a single night.

This collection offers the obvious advantage of minimal cost compared to later potential rewards.

Toys

Anthropologists and historians tell us that every society has had some form of toys for children. If collecting itself is just a form of play, then any student of psychology can venture a guess as to why toys are a popular collectible. All indications point to toys as a continued area of growth.

Toys of the eighteenth century are truly museum pieces and are currently too overpriced to be considered future collectibles. In addition, only the most skilled individual can detect the fake from the real antique. By the later part of the nineteenth century metal replaced wood as the common toy material. But it is actually the toys of the last fifty years that offer the greatest opportunity for dramatic price increases.

Like all types of collectibles, toy fashions change. The following represent the best potentials for appreciation.

CURRENT TOYS NOW BEING MANUFACTURED
(In Order of Investment Quality):
1. Space toys (especially *Star Wars* toys, ray guns, helmets, and mechanical spaceships)
2. Trucks, cars, and trains
3. Model soldiers

OLDER TOYS WORTH ACQUIRING
(In Order of Investment Quality):
1. British tin toys (e.g., Hornby Dinky toys)
2. Steel lithography (e.g., pail and shovel)
3. Toy china

A wealth of playthings form this category, but we will mention just a few: cars, banks, wind-up toys, balls, marbles, and toy figurines.

NAME	DATE	DESCRIPTION	CURRENT PRICE
Barney Google & Spark Plug	1920s	Reproductions of cartoon characters; jointed wooden bodies	up to $100 each
Boss Tweed bank	1870s	Mechanical bank with latticework on chair (Boss seems to stick coin in inside pocket)	$125–$300

NAME	DATE	DESCRIPTION	CURRENT PRICE
Camel on wheels	1800s	Tin pull toy with bell	up to $580
Carpet ball	late 1800s	Colorful ceramic balls used for rolling on carpets	$50–$60 each
Glass marbles	unknown	2-inch marbles, with elaborate color "swirls" inside	up to $40 each
Hansom cab (Pratt & Letchworth Co.)	1910	Pull toy of horse, cab, and driver	up to $750
Indian & Bear bank	1910	Cast iron (Indian shoots coin inside bear)	up to $325
Ives train	1890s	Cast iron, five cars	$300–$400
Marx Merry-makers	1930s	Wind-up tin mouse band	up to $150
Mickey Mouse watch	1933	Mickey Mouse face with original strap and box	up to $200
Pinocchio figurines	1930s	Bisque Woolworth figures	$18–$20 each (originally 5¢)
Studebaker pedal car	1925	4½-foot metal car, with moving gadgets	up to $700

Victorian Paperweights

Glass paperweights were introduced in the middle 1800s. Their colorful floral designs immediately appealed to Victorians; easier travel and less expensive postage, made them common objects, found in many homes.

The glassware technique, dating back to the first century, was studied and relearned by European glassmakers. By the middle of the nineteenth century, glass paperweights, ink and scent bottles, seals, vases, and bowls were in abundant supply.

Paperweights were the favorite item among these objects. They were made by encasing in glass a design of tiny, colored glass rods. This design was held in place while layers of glass were added to achieve the desired size and magnification. Varying glass consistencies, or dust particles trapped in the creative processes, would show as flaws in the finished product.

Today these imperfections will decrease the paperweight's value. Other factors affecting value are neatness of design, brilliance of colors, and the clarity of the glass. For maximum value, paperweights from this era must be in mint condition.

As with all collectibles, value will also be determined by scarcity and rarity. Paperweight manufacturing was at its height from 1845 to 1855, and again, in America, from 1852 to 1875. Since then many paperweights have been sold to museum collections, or simply been lost and broken. Originally these paperweights sold for just a few dollars. Today an authentic piece, in mint condition, may sell for as much as $20,400.

Here is a list of a few, authentic Victorian paperweight designs and their manufacturers.

DESIGN	MANUFACTURER	YEARS MADE
Bouquet	Saint Louis	1845–55
Daisies	France	late 19th century
Flowers	America	late 19th century
Lily of the Valley	Saint Louis	1845–55
Millefiori	Clichy	1845–55
Millefiori with Overlay	Clichy	1845–55
Pink Rose	France	late 19th century
Pansy	Baccarat	1845–55
Portrait of Napoleon	Clichy	1845–55
Queen Victoria	Clichy	1845–55
Six-Looped Garland	Clichy	1845–55
Three Strawberries	Baccarat	1845–55

Generally, the above paperweights are available only at the extremely high price of $300 and up. Watch out for fakes; reproductions are often very good and can fool even an experienced dealer.

Appendices I to IV

Appendix I:

Magazines, Periodicals, and Newsletters on Collectibles

Where do you get the most recent information on prices? How can you keep pace with the latest trends? Where can you learn about meetings and conventions? Where do you discover what's being issued?

The answer to all of these questions is: in the periodical that best suits your interest. If you're like most people, you'll need at least two subscriptions to cover the range of your interests.

What follows is a list of the latest magazines and periodicals. We suggest that you write for several sample issues to see which ones best meet your individual needs.

Acquire
170 Fifth Avenue
New York, New York 10010

(One year, 5 issues—$8.50)

American Antiques
Lindencroft Publications
R.D. 1, Box 241
New Hope, Pennsylvania 18938

(One year—$8)

American Collector
Real Resources Group, Box A
Reno, Nevada 89506

(One year—$7.98)

Antique Gazette
929 Davidson Drive
Nashville, Tennessee 37205

(One year—$5)

Antique Monthly
P.O. Drawer 2
Tuscaloosa, Alabama 35401

(One year—$11)

Antiques
551 Fifth Avenue
New York, New York 10017

(One year—$24)

Antiques and the Arts Weekly
The Bee Publishing Company
Newton, Connecticut 06470

(One year—$6.50)

Antiques and Auction News
Box B
Marietta, Pennsylvania 17547

(One year—$6)

The Antiques Journal
Box 1046
Dubuque, Iowa 52001

(One year—$7.95)

The Antique Trader Weekly
Box 1050
Dubuque, Iowa 52001

(One year—$11)

Chesapeake Antique Journal
Box 500
Warwick, Maryland 21912

(One year—$8.50)

Circa
P.O. Box 924, Barrie
Ontario, Canada L4M-4Y6

(One year, 11 issues—$7.50)

The Collector
Drawer C
Kermit, Texas 79745

(One year—$7.50)

Collector-Antiquer
4 South Main Street
Pittsford, New York 14534

(One year—$5)

Collectors News
606 Eighth Street
Grundy Center, Iowa 50638

(One year—$7.50)

Depression Glass Daze
Box 57C
Otisville, Michigan 48463

(One year—$5.50)

The Drummer
Unadilla Forks
West Winfield, New York 13491

(One year, 24 issues—$5)

Hobbies
Lightner Publishing Corporation
1006 South Michigan Avenue
Chicago, Illinois 60605

(One year—$7)

The Jersey Devil
New Egypt Auction and Farmers Market
Route 537
New Egypt, New Jersey 08533

(One year—$3)

Maine Antique Digest
Box 358, Jefferson Street
Waldoboro, Maine 04572

(One year—$7.50)

The Miniature Collector
Acquire Publishing Company
170 Fifth Avenue
New York, New York 10010

(One year—$12)

National Antiques Review
P.O. Box 619
Portland, Maine 04104

(One year—$7.50)

National Depression Glass Journal
Box 268
Billings, Montana 65610

(One year—$5)

The New York Antique Almanac
P.O. Box 335
Lawrence, New York 11559

(One year—$6)

Ohio Antiques Review
P.O. Box 538
Worthington, Ohio 43085

(One year—$7)

Price Guide to Antiques
The Babka Publishing Company
P.O. Box 1050
Dubuque, Iowa 52001

(One year—$6)

Relics
Western Publications, Inc.
P.O. Box 3338
Austin, Texas 78764

(One year—$2.50)

Spinning Wheel
Fame Avenue
Hanover, Pennsylvania 17331

(One year—$9)

Tri-State Trader
27 North Jefferson Street
Knightstown, Indiana 46148

(One year—$7.50)

Appendix II:

Collectors' Clubs You Can Join

Beer Can Collectors of America
7500 Devonshire
St. Louis, Missouri 63119

Tin Container Collectors' Association
P.O. Box 4555
Denver, Colorado 80204

Mechanical Bank Collectors of America
c/o Albert Davidson
905 Manor Lane
Bayshore, New York 11706

National Button Society of America
1132 Dunwoody Drive
Kirkwood, Missouri 63123

American Numismatic Association
P.O. Box 2366
Colorado Springs, Colorado 80901

International Doll Association
10920 Indian Trail, Suite 302
Dallas, Texas 75229

United Federation of Doll Clubs, Inc.
137 Hendricks Boulevard
Buffalo, New York 14226

Chicago Playing Card Collectors
9645 South Leavitt Street
Chicago, Illinois 60643

International Carnival Glass Association
3142 South 35th Street
LaCross, Wisconsin 54601

National Early American Glass Club
31 Norwood Street
Sharon, Massachusetts 02067

Pewter Collectors' Club of America
P.O. Box 239
Saugerties, New York 12477

American Model Soldier and American
Military Historical Society
1524 El Camino Real
San Carlos, California 94070

Miniature Figure Collectors of America
Box 311
Haverford, Pennsylvania 19041

National Association of Miniature Enthusiasts
P.O. Box 2621
Anaheim, California 92804

National Sheet Music Society, Inc.
P.O. Box 2235
Pasadena, California 91105

United in Group Harmony Association
(Collectors of 1950s records)
P.O. Box 185
Clifton, New Jersey 07011

National Stereoscopic Association
R.D. 1, Box 426A
Fremont, New Hampshire 03044

American Political Item Collectors
66 Golf Street
Newington, Connecticut 06111

Association for the Preservation of Political Americana
P.O. Box 211
Forest Hills, New York 11375

National Political Button Exchange
530 Yosemite Avenue
Mountain View, California 94040

Deltiologists of America
(Collectors of picture postcards)
3709 Gradyville Road
Newton Square, Pennsylvania 19073

International Postcard Collectors Association
6380 Wilshire Boulevard, Suite 907
Los Angeles, California 90048

Nostalgia Collectors' Club
440 West 34th Street (1A)
New York, New York 10001

National Friends of Rare Porcelain
1911 Boardwalk
Atlantic City, New Jersey 08401

Railroadians of America
43 Hillcrest Road
Madison, New Jersey 07940

Rough & Tumble Engineers' Historical Association
Lincoln Highway
Kinzers, Pennsylvania 17535

Midwest Sports Collectors' Association
c/o Jay Barry
15261 Northfield
Oak Park, Michigan 48237

The American Philatelic Society, Inc.
Box 800
State College, Pennsylvania 16801

U.S. Cancellation Club
855 Cove Way
Denver, Colorado 80209

Early American Industries Association
Division of Historical Services
Building #8, Rotterdam Industrial Park
Schenectady, New York 12306

Early Trades and Crafts Society
60 Harves Lane
Levittown, New York 11756

Texas Barbed Wire Collectors Association
4013 Ridgelea Drive
Austin, Texas 78331

International Toy Buffs' Association
425 East Green Street, Room 500 W.
Pasadena, California 91103

Antique Automobile Club of America
West Derry Road
Hershey, Pennsylvania 17033

Antique Bicycle Club of America
260 West 260th Street
Bronx, New York 10471

The Carriage Association of America
855 Forest Avenue
Portland, Maine 04103

Horseless Carriage Club
9031 East Florence Avenue
Downey, California 90240

Victorian Society of America
Athenaeum of Philadelphia
East Washington Square
Philadelphia, Pennsylvania 19106

National Association of Watch and Clock Collectors
P.O. Box 33
Columbia, Pennsylvania 17512

Appendix III:

Your Collection Chart

Every true collector should keep careful records of every item in his collection. This can be done casually or carefully, though naturally we prefer the latter. To help you begin, we suggest the chart on the pages that follow.

This chart is designed for the general collector. Each individual should attempt to edit, modify, and change this chart so that it best suits his or her own needs.

One additional suggestion: Once this chart has been set up and maintained on an up-to-date basis, you should make an extra copy to keep in your bank vault in case of fire. It could be the type of record your insurance company requires when it comes time to verify a loss.

YOUR COLLECTION CHART

ITEM	DATE PURCHASED	WHERE PURCHASED	PURCHASE PRICE	ESTIMATED CURRENT VALUE	IDENTIFYING MARKS	ARTIST OR CRAFTSMAN

YOUR COLLECTION CHART

ITEM	DATE PURCHASED	WHERE PURCHASED	PURCHASE PRICE	ESTIMATED CURRENT VALUE	IDENTIFYING MARKS	ARTIST OR CRAFTSMAN

Appendix IV:

Three Lists to Help You
Pick an Area of Collection

The first of these lists is designed to reveal those items you should never consider collecting. Why? Because they will probably never go up in value. The second list contains items that may possibly rise in value but with no certainty. You may consider going into these types of collectibles if you're willing to invest in something fairly chancy. The third lists those items we feel have the strongest potential for the future.

Of course, there are no guarantees. Flukes do happen, and there are sudden fads that run contrary to all logic. It's important to remember, too, that there can be both rapid growth and rapid decline within any category; individual items are always more important than a category. Watch out for those who give the blanket advice, "Invest in stamps," for surely some stamps today are underpriced and others are overpriced. Before committing large sums of money you would be wise to study your chosen category in depth.

You may be surprised what I have listed in some of the following categories. For example, the text indicates spectacular rises in coin prices, yet they are listed in only the medium value group. Herein lies the secret of collecting *tomorrow's* collectibles. First, just because an item has shown an upward, trend do not be misled into thinking that trend must continue. Second, the prices of some items have reached their peak. Third, it is my firm belief that the most dramatic rises will take place in the lower-priced items. It is an economic theory of collecting that an increase in price from $50 to $500 is far more easily accomplished than one from $200 to $1,000.

Therefore, an individual with $1,000 in available investment funds may be better off investing in lower-priced items. The caveat is this—learn to distinguish between a low-priced item with potential and just plain junk that will never appreciate.

LOW-VALUE COLLECTIBLES
(Look for little or no appreciation)

Clothing
Current United States commemorative stamps
Collectibles issued by private mints
Plates (especially privately produced, expensive limited
    editions)
Sport stars' autographs
Spoons

MEDIUM-VALUE COLLECTIBLES

Comics
Dolls
Glass paperweights
Theater programs
Advertising items, especially premiums
Coins

HIGH-VALUE COLLECTIBLES

Elvis Presley records
Miniatures
Space toys
First-edition books
Autographs of political figures